COMBAT CONTRAILS VIETNAM

William B. Scott

A North Slope Publications Book
PUBLISHED BY NORTH SLOPE PUBLICATIONS

North Slope Publications

A North Slope Publications Book

PUBLISHED BY NORTH SLOPE PUBLICATIONS

COMBAT CONTRAILS VIETNAM by William B. Scott
Published by North Slope Publications
Colorado

Copyright © 2021 by William B. Scott
All rights reserved, including the right to reproduce this book,
or portions thereof, in any form.

*Cover design by Jim "Hazy" Haseltine,
HIGH-G Technologies/HIGH-G Productions (high-g.com)
Page layout design by Lisa Caputo*

Visit the author's website at www.williambscott.com

Library of Congress Cataloging-in-Publication Data
Scott, Bill, 1946-

Combat Contrails Vietnam/William B. Scott

ISBN 978-0-9842063-8-4 (trade paper)
1. American history-Vietnam. Nonfiction
2. Military Arts and Science. Nonfiction.

First Edition September 2021.

Dedicated to the Warriors of Vietnam,
who answered their nation's call.

I have done things that haunt me at night, so you can sleep in peace.
I have been away from my family a long time, so that yours can be safe.
I have sacrificed a lot of my life, so that you may live free.
I have done these things, because I have sworn an oath to my country.
And I will live by this oath, until the day I die,
because I am and always will be a…
U.S. VETERAN

Vince Forbes

INTRODUCTION
William B. Scott

I was moved to write COMBAT CONTRAILS: VIETNAM, after hearing many friends' stories, few of which had been captured in print. After several of those men passed away, it became acutely evident that Vietnam veterans are aging and departing at an ever-increasing rate.

Recent high-profile books have honored World War II and Iraq/Afghanistan veterans, but many of those who fought in Vietnam have been overlooked or ignored. Yes, a few veterans have written superb fiction and nonfiction books about combat in Vietnam. However, far too many vets are going to the grave, taking untold stories with them.

Although a Vietnam-era vet, I didn't fly in-country. But I witnessed the demeaning nastiness dozens of friends and colleagues suffered, when they returned to the states. Spit upon, called baby killers and branded as racist—or worse—those warriors simply clammed up and never talked about their war, the messy one America supposedly lost and wanted to forget.

The Vietnam War years were divisive, tumultuous, deadly and seemingly endless. Nevertheless, thousands of Americans stepped up and did what the nation's leaders demanded, regardless of how utterly senseless their missions might have been. It's high time we honor those warriors, by capturing their stories to inform subsequent generations.

Most vets I approached agreed to share their wartime experiences. Understandably, others declined, opting to not relive them. All could relate to sentiments perfectly expressed by U.S. Navy combat aviator and bestselling author, Stephen Coonts:

"But combat stuff... Most of that shit has faded. Old age, I suppose. Don't think about it for forty or fifty years and it becomes static inside the brain. Fortunately for me I captured my memories while they were fresh and I was younger in FLIGHT OF THE INTRUDER. Night cat shots, the marshal pattern circling to hit the fix at the exact time to commence the descent to the ship, getting launched in the tanker to hawk the last recovery, which was always fucked up after a long day of combat and shitty weather. Getting shot at, watching the flak come up as I raced along at 250 feet, or 300, watching SAMs lift off and level off and come down toward me...the

flak curtains; sitting in the ready room smoking, soaked in a wet flight suit, so damn tired I didn't want to get out of the chair, just happy to be alive.... I remember that, but the details have sort of turned to electronic static. Maybe that's good. Remember the good stuff and forget the bad shit. Remember how the experience felt...even if the details have faded."

Hang tough,
Steve Coonts
1-19-21

ARE YOU READY?
Stephen Coonts

Grumman A-6 Intruder
U.S. Navy

Are you ready to die today?

Every man or woman who goes into combat must answer that question or try to evade it.

When I was a young A-6 pilot aboard USS Enterprise during the final years of the Vietnam War, we suited up for every mission in a locker room. The lockers were in a bank of lockers presumably stolen from some distant high school or purchased as surplus when the high school upgraded. Our flight gear hung in our lockers, so we took it out, waved it around to try to dissipate the smell, and put it on. G-suit, torso harness with survival vest, belt and holster for the pistol, helmet bag with oxygen mask... When we had it all on, we were ready to waddle to the ladder or escalator that took us to the flight-deck level, where we would enter the aircraft handler's domain to find out where on the flight deck our steeds were parked, and to certify the weight for the catapult shot.

But in the locker room before we donned all that flight gear, each of us took a moment to empty the pockets of our flight suits into the locker.

Our wallets, of course, the wedding ring if we had one, and anything else of a personal nature, such as letters from parents, girlfriends or wives. Each of us looked at his little pile on the top shelf of his locker and wondered if today was his day. Will I ever see this stuff again? Will I die today? Or tonight, since the A-6 Intruder was designed as a low-level night bomber and in the final year of the war we used it that way.

Are you ready to die today?

If you were flying a daytime Alpha Strike into North Vietnam you would be in a formation, trying hard to stay with your leader, listening to the voices on the radio scream of SAMs flying, perhaps MiGs, and bitching about the clouds in the target area. Of course the bad guys would be shooting, but you wouldn't be able to see the flak while you flew formation. If you were hit you'd know it pretty quick, and if your airplane began to die, you would know that too. But were you ready to die today?

If you were going on a single-plane night strike, you would be flying as low as you dared while the bombardier-navigator (BN) beside you worked the radar and computer to find the target and the flak spewed up from the earth in long, red ribbons, curving behind you as you raced along at 480 knots, a few hundred feet above the paddies and trees with a load of bombs. But for every tracer there were five artillery shells that weren't tracer; the night sky was full of steel. Will I die tonight?

If you were flying the night tanker, you would need every flying skill you possessed to tank the nervous pilots having trouble getting aboard, then get aboard yourself when you had given away all your fuel, when the ship was pitching and rolling in a heaving sea under a low ceiling as rain pelted down and all your squadron mates were in the ready room getting settled for a movie. It would be just you and your BN in that little cockpit as you worked the stick and throttles to get aboard where others had failed.

Today, tonight, are you ready?

Are you ready to meet your maker?

Death in airplanes happens really fast and is probably painless, an instant transition from this life to the next. If there is a next, and you and your Creator can commune about that.

But are you ready to go? Have you told your loved ones that you care? Are you ready to face whatever comes?

Truly, any day in anyone's life can be their last. Freak accidents, car wrecks, heart attacks happen with monotonous regularity, even if they are rare. Sooner or later it might be your turn. Sooner or later it will be your turn. Of course, you know that if there is any dying to be done today or tonight it will be the other fellow; you'll live to the age of 95, die in bed, be shot to death by a jealous husband. But. Maybe, just maybe, perhaps it won't be the other guy tonight. Are you ready?

In combat the opposition is trying to kill you. Every warrior understands that basic truth and must come to grips with it. Most people can. We are all going to die; the only question is when. A few people freeze when faced with a situation that is more dangerous than jaywalking. You can't freeze in combat.

As you stand there at your locker stowing your wallet and your wedding ring, you must answer the question: Am I ready?

Put on your flight gear, ride the escalator to the flight deck, and tell the handler how much your airplane weighs. Then go out onto that dark, windy flight deck to meet the airplane that may be your coffin.

Yes, Lord, I am ready.

I was born ready.

Dan Bayer

Stephen Coonts is the author of innumerable New York Times bestsellers, the first of which was the classic combat tale, Flight of the Intruder.

He majored in political science at West Virginia University, graduating in 1968 with an A.B. degree. Upon graduation, he was commissioned an

Ensign in the U.S. Navy and began flight training in Pensacola, Florida. He received his Navy wings in August, 1969, completed fleet replacement training in the A-6 Intruder aircraft and reported to Attack Squadron 196 at NAS Whidbey Island, Washington. He made two combat cruises aboard USS Enterprise during the final years of the Vietnam War as a member of this squadron. After the war, he served as a flight instructor on A-6 aircraft for two years, then did a tour as an assistant catapult and arresting gear officer aboard USS Nimitz. He left active duty in 1977 and moved to Colorado. After short stints as a taxi driver and police officer, he entered the University of Colorado School of Law and received his law degree in December, 1979.

His first novel, Flight of the Intruder, published in September 1986 by the Naval Institute Press, spent 28 weeks on the New York Times bestseller lists in hardcover. A motion picture based on this novel, with the same title, was released nationwide in January 1991.

The U.S. Naval Institute honored him with its Author of the Year Award for the year 1986 for his novel, Flight of the Intruder. He was a trustee of West Virginia Wesleyan College from 1990-1998, and was inducted into the West Virginia University Academy of Distinguished Alumni in 1992. In 2014 West Virginia University awarded him an honorary Doctor of Letters degree.

STEEL STORM: A Pivotal Battle Kept Secret to Protect a President*

William B. Scott

28-29 July 1965

Where the hell are you, Charlie? You're out there. I feel it.

A rawboned, lanky U.S. Marine strained to detect movement in the inky darkness, a starless space made blacker by a rain squall that suppressed the sounds of soldiers creeping toward their objective. A few feet away, a South Vietnamese Ranger, Sergeant Thi, also patrolled, straining to spot a large Viet Cong force they knew was approaching. An attack was imminent.

As he scouted the area, Corporal Karl Lippard mentally took inventory of his dicey situation and limited assets. He was armed with an M14 rifle and four 20-round magazines. Sgt. Thi carried a .30-caliber M1 carbine, and a Colt 1911 semiautomatic pistol was tucked into his M9 shoulder holster. The Marine had stowed his map case, helmet, poncho and pack in an old French bunker near the Ca De River bridge's north approach. A telephone land line linked the abandoned bunker to roughly 20 other Marines dug-in on the south side. All were "Raiders", a company of U.S. Marines that had received specialized training—"rubber boat" operations and submarine insertion, for example. Raiders were elite forces, the handpicked best of each U. S. Marine Corps battalion.

As the rain squall intensified, Lippard and Thi returned to the French bunker to retrieve their ponchos. A South Vietnamese army (ARVN) soldier was manning the concrete shelter, talking on a PRC-10 backpack radio...but to Viet Cong troops. Lippard pulled the pin on a grenade and placed a hand on the bunker wall, but before he could take out the VC infiltrator, Sgt. Thi tossed his own grenade. Its blast cut the enemy soldier in half, severed the phone line and drove debris into Lippard's knee.

"My grenade was live, still in my hand, when I got hit," Lippard recalled. "Had to replace the pin." The Marine stepped inside the bunker, confirmed the VC was a goner and checked the PRC-10 radio. It was covered in blood and raw flesh, but still functional.

That radio would become his lifeline.

Positioned on the north side of the Ca De River, which emptied into nearby Bay of Da Nang, Lippard was acutely aware that he and his Vietnamese Ranger sidekick were mere tripwires, a flesh-and-blood early warning system. The 19-year-old Marine had orders to sound a warning, if anybody approached the bridge from the north. Nobody—friend or foe—would be permitted to cross.

Had the VC mole alerted nearby enemy troops that the bridge was defended by a pitifully small force? No way of knowing, but the grenade blast that had silenced him surely would attract Charlie's attention to the old bunker.

In fact, Lippard wasn't "officially" in that bunker on the Ca De River's north bank. Then-Major General Lewis W. Walt's Tactical Area of Responsibility ended on the south end of a five-span, quarter-mile steel structure. With a set of railroad tracks down the center and pedestrian walkway along the west side, the bridge was a critical north-south artery. "Highway One" and a railroad converged at that crossing, a gateway to the main route linking "Da Nang to places north, such as Phu Bai and Hue," according to the record of a ship soon to be anchored nearby, in the bay.

Holding that junction was absolutely vital. Regimental commander Colonel Edwin B. Wheeler had told 2nd Lieutenant James Reeder, Lippard's immediate commander, "Lieutenant, if you lose this bridge, you and I are both going to be fired." But holding it from only the south end was tactically near-impossible.

"There was no room to support Marines on the south side," Lippard recalled. "The available space [there] could only hold about 20 Marines. Besides, that's about all that could be spared. We were spread real thin in July 1965."

To have any serious hope of preventing enemy troops from taking the bridge, a full company of Marines, backed by artillery, should have been firmly entrenched on the north side. But bizarre rules of engagement in mid-1965 placed responsibility for defending that important span's northerly approach in the hands of a South Vietnamese army battalion located about a half mile farther north, close to the beach. Comprising two under-strength platoons, these "Popular Force" troops were a battalion in name only, a reserve unit commanded by a schoolteacher. They were volunteers, designated the Army of the Republic of Vietnam (ARVN) 2nd Regional Force.

A USMC battalion would be composed of 1,000 Marines. In contrast, "a Vietnamese 'battalion' would indicate 600 or more men," Lippard explained. "Years later, we found documents [proving] the ARVN 2nd was only a couple of platoons, mostly farmers. Weekend warriors, often with families in tow. But two platoons of drop-and-run farmers wouldn't cut it, if hit. That 'battalion' would be wiped out."

Lippard and Thi knew little about Viet Cong movements in the area or the unit set to attack the bridge that night. They had been given no intelligence, even though 3rd Marine headquarters was well-aware that the 7th Viet Cong Battalion had slipped between the Bay of Da Nang and a ridge of mountains the day before. Two Marine companies had been dispatched to engage that force, but they never encountered the 7th VC. It had already passed through, pushing to the north.

Records indicate that Navy ships positioned offshore had "tried to interdict this battalion, shelling its [potential] positions, as it moved," Lippard said. A combat action report noted the 7th VC was still maneuvering on 28 July, arriving in a valley a few miles north of the Ca De River bridge late that day.

Well after sunset, two separate formations, each comprising two companies of Viet Cong and Red Chinese regulars, started moving south. Their apparent plan was to sweep across the Ca De River bridge, overrun a 3rd Marine Division command post and capture the huge Da Nang airbase 4.5 miles west of the city.

"Confirmed," Lippard asserted. "There were [a total of] 16,516 Viet

Cong against 1,140 men of 2nd Battalion, 4th Marines, in open, fixed positions. They'd be overwhelmed, with no support," if squeezed by enemy troops from the north and south. The enemy would have destroyed innumerable aircraft, including helicopters slated to support a major battle shaping up at Chu Lai, well to the south.

"The Fourth Marines would have been doomed," Lippard declared. "Another 1,121 Marines—the First of the Fourth—on the beach to the northeast at Ky Ha would have been next. General Walt could see it coming. His [planned] strike at Chu Lai…would be preempted by that VC offensive [launched] at the Ca De River bridge. He had no real protection. No one to come to his aid. Therefore, he sent what he had to the bridge and hoped for the best."

Conceivably, the 7th VC—about 600 strong—would race down to Chu Lai, attacking from behind and wiping out that assembling American force of some 1,140 men.

The only speed bumps were a Marine and ARVN Ranger holed up near a bunker on the north end of the bridge, backed by 20 lightly armed Marines on the south side. It's safe to assume that 7th VC commanders fully expected to swat that handful of Marines aside and be in control of Da Nang air base before dawn on 29 July.

Clearly, U.S. commanders were anticipating an attack from the northwest by a massive VC force in the Da Nang operations area. On 1 July, Marine Division headquarters had issued an order warning of precisely that possibility. A subsequent missive on 17 July approved naval gunfire support (NGS) for in-country employment, albeit with constraints. Supporting fire had to be "observed and controlled," called in by only U.S. forces, and independent fire from any ship offshore was banned.

Something big was about to happen, but Lippard had no idea what. Around 2100 (9:00 p.m. local), "we began to receive enemy fire from several directions [near] the bunker, increasing in intensity as I tried to raise somebody on the radio," he said. Only one faint response was received—a patrol some five miles up-river. It was unable to relay a message.

"A Mayday call went out to any station on the net," Lippard recounted. "Division headquarters came up, and I quickly gave them positions of attacking forces, while I could." He noted that the enemy was "Danger close!" No artillery was available, so aircraft were dispatched. Soon, USMC F-4B Phantoms from Da Nang air base arrived and made three strikes on coordinates

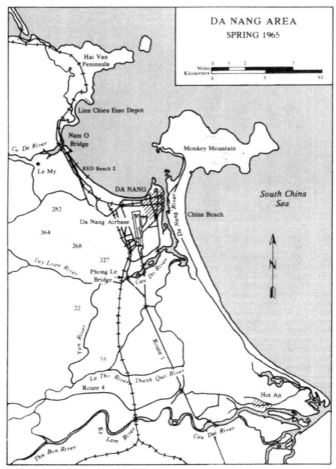

Da Nang operations area. Battle of the Ca De River bridge occurred in the upper left.

Lippard provided, pounding rear elements of the 7th VC Battalion.

"Division never identified themselves. Never said what, if anything, they were sending," Lippard said. He was told to identify himself, "but I declined to give my position. Evidently satisfied, they sent everything they had—aircraft and ships." One U.S. Navy ship steamed for several hours to get on-station. "So division knew they were in trouble. They also knew somebody on the other end of that radio [link] could read a map and was under fire. A heavy firefight was in progress."

Seasoned enemy soldiers intent on clearing the French bunker and sprinting across the bridge were hardly deterred by three rapid-fire F-4 strikes. The 7th's troops kept coming, and Lippard and Sgt. Thi kept picking them off, when briefly illuminated by lightning.

In short order, Lippard had shot and killed 15-20 enemy soldiers with his M14. "They were attacking in threes, so we could take them down fairly quickly." Sgt. Thi ran out of M1 ammunition, prompting Lippard to trade his M14 and extra ammo magazines for Thi's .45-caliber pistol. The Marine could fire the forty-five one-handed and still operate the PRC-10 radio, his only means of communication.

Fortuitously, Lippard happened to be an expert shot with a forty-five. Years later, he would set world records for nailing targets at 500, 600 and 1,000 yards with the "Combat NCO," a .45-caliber semiautomatic of his own design.

With enemy fire zeroed-in on the old bunker, Lippard and Thi abandoned it, moved about 75 yards up the beach, and took cover behind sand dunes, backs to the water. Lippard radioed a brief situation report (SITREP) to division headquarters, which merely acknowledged that artillery couldn't reach him, then went silent.

"No further transmission. None from them or me. I was busy," Lippard clipped. The young Marine was on his own. Reinforcements and artillery simply weren't available. He transmitted in the blind, "Mayday! Mayday! Mayday! Any station this net! This is Hotel Three! Do you copy? Over!"

"Hotel Three, this is Assassin. Give me your coordinates." Out there in the Da Nang Bay, just offshore, a very powerful ally was arriving.

Answering Lippard's call was Harry Rodgers RD2, a sailor aboard the USS John R. Craig (DD-885), a U.S. Navy destroyer sporting four five-inch guns, two on its forward deck and another two on the aft. Rodgers was tasked with maintaining communications between the ship and a "target spotter" ashore. He received and plotted target coordinates as requested by the spotter. Those were passed to the ship Gunnery Officer, who fed them into a fire control computer and unleashed the guns. The spotter—Lippard, in this case—would call for illumination, high-explosive or white phosphorus rounds and make target adjustments, as required.

Navy gun support tactics in mid-1965 were to "get in as close to shore as possible, drop anchor and maneuver [to] bring guns to bear, while swinging on the anchor chain," according to the Craig's history. The ship drew about 18 feet of water and was now anchored in about 25 feet. Crewmembers said the Craig's propellers were churning up bottom mud to keep

USS John R. Craig (DD-885)

the ship broadside to the beach, ensuring both fore and aft five-inch gun mounts could provide supporting fire.

By 2141 (9:41 p.m. local), the Craig was in position, lights out, and starting to fire illumination rounds, directed by Lippard's radio calls. Now, "I could see the [enemy] force…but was unaware that a whole battalion was engaging," the Marine recalls. "The Craig came in [and started firing] to the right of the airstrikes, immediately across my front, giving me some relief."

Once he realized a huge Viet Cong/Red Chinese force was caught in the open, lit up by the Craig's first illumination rounds, Lippard requested high-explosive shells. "I called the first rounds within 100 yards" of his and Thi's beach position. "If I had not retired to the beach, I would have died at the bridge. It was very bad on the beach, but the dunes [absorbed] a lot, and as the enemy fell back, concussions from naval gunfire and [incoming] enemy fire decreased."

Noise from airbursts was deafening, complicating radio communications. As Lippard shot enemy soldiers closing on his position, he transmitted a steady stream of radio calls, directing the big guns' devastating fire. High explosive rounds "were tight" and accurate. The advantages of heavy rain and pitch darkness that enemy commanders had counted on for concealment were eradicated by frequent illumination rounds turning night into day.

Up the beach, the South Vietnamese reserves "were digging to China, pinned against the sea. [The Craig's incessant barrage] had them bottled up and afraid to move," Lippard said. "They had no idea who was calling in the fire or where it was coming from."

Illumination rounds enabled Lippard and Thi spotting and shooting enemy troops "that made it to within fifteen yards of us. It was close; very, very close," the Marine distinctly remembers. "The 'problem' was danger close that night. I was down to just my pistol, and plotted the last rounds right on my position. [We] could not hold, without maximum firepower on me. We got lucky."

Lippard was a reluctant student, when assigned to Map and Aerial Photo School in his early Marine Corps days, yet graduated at the top of his class. On the night of 28-29 July 1965, he was grateful for training-honed skills that enabled calling in absolutely devastating fire for almost five hours. The USS Craig ultimately fired 340 five-inch rounds—57 illumination, 22 white phosphorous and 261 high-explosive shells.

At 0146 (1:46 a.m.) on 29 July, the USS Stoddard (DD-566) slipped into Da Nang Bay and joined the battle. Lippard was unaware that two ships were firing through the night. He simply called the coordinates and that zone was obliterated. "They answered a Marine corporal's Mayday. No questions."

Relentless pounding by two Navy destroyers' five-inch guns forced the Vietcong and Red Chinese regulars to "collapse on themselves. I followed up the beach as enemy troops [dropped back], then inland as they retraced their approach of march," Lippard continued. Approaching the ARVN reserves' position, "Sgt. Thi broke off to identify me on their flank. I moved inland, following the enemy and [directing naval] gunfire. I was then forty-five yards forward of the ARVN position." The Marine was alone in no-man's land, surrounded by dead enemy soldiers…or what was left of them. Lippard doesn't talk about that.

When the Craig and Stoddard ceased firing, "I retired back to the beach and retraced my movements to the point of first call [for naval gunfire]. There I remained until daylight." The Craig was ordered to weigh anchor and depart around 0310 (3:10 a.m.), but the Stoddard remained in Da Nang Bay until about 10:00 a.m. "The battle was over, but she finished some mop-up, [shelling] the base of the mountains [to take out] any stragglers or other units that might arrive."

Records of the battle are sketchy and don't always agree, but Lippard's research found that 443 shells were fired by the Craig and Stoddard in response to his Mayday calls the night of 28-29 July 1965. Another 33 were delivered during post-battle mop-up operations. Ship logs have ambigu-

USS Stoddard

ous accounts, including numbers that don't match other records: the USS John R. Craig—under the command of Navy Commander James Kenneth Jobe and supported by Lieutenant Jeremy Michael Boorda, the Weapons Officer—fired 340 rounds, while "conducting a night firing mission." How many the USS Stoddard delivered under the command of U.S. Navy Commander Charles Presgrove is believed to be 95 rounds in the early morning hours of 29 July, and another 174 in ill-defined "after-action" operations, according to a Naval War Gunfire Support Record.

A personal log written by Henry Lehtola, an enlisted sailor-turned-historian who chronicled the Craig's role in the 28-29 July 1965 battle for the Ca De Bridge, backs Lippard's account: "Anchored Da Nang. ...preparing to open fire. The VC must have been raising hell earlier. You could hear small arms fire on the beach and see tracers flying. Flares and star shells lit up the whole sky."

The U.S. Marine Corps War Journal's cursory documentation for 28 July notes, "USS Craig commenced firing on designated targets. 340 five-inch rounds expended—57 illumination; 22 white phosphorous, and 261 high explosive. At 0146 hr., Craig joined by USS Stoddard (DD-566) in support."

Although exhausted, Corporal Karl Lippard jotted down a few notes about the night's battle and had his knee wound dressed. Later, he snapped several color photos, then waited, fully expecting a thorough debriefing by his commanders. It didn't happen. Nobody at headquarters ever asked for Lippard's account, verbal or written.

Senior Marine commanders definitely knew the intense Ca De River bridge battle had occurred. In fact, the USS Craig and Stoddard destroyers would not have steamed into Da Nang Bay in response to Lippard's Mayday call, unless ordered by the Commanding General of Naval Forces,

The USS Craig's scorched 5-inch gun barrels and expended brass.

Major General Walt. However, 3rd Marine headquarters apparently never reported the engagement's stark truth: A single USMC Raider, aided by an ARVN Ranger, directed naval gun fire on a battalion-size unit of enemy soldiers caught in the open. After about five hours of intense bombardment, the Viet Cong 7th Battalion ceased to exist. No enemy soldiers captured. No wounded recovered. No sign that any of the unit's approximately 600 Viet Cong and Red Chinese combatants had escaped. The VC 7th simply vanished, never to reappear in subsequent reports.

Incredibly, not a single Marine or ARVN soldier was killed. "Right. No Marine or ARVN losses," Lippard confirmed.

"The end result of this battle was total destruction of the 7th Viet Cong Battalion, by U.S. Marines in defense of the bridge complex," Lippard recapped. "The Marine Corps acted with speed and force—brought in Marine Air Wing strikes and quickly moved Navy ships into position to provide full gun support within minutes of my call. …This is believed to be one of the finest examples of combined Navy and Marine assets…in support of a small unit, during the Vietnam War."

Although U.S. commanders may have ignored or forgotten the Ca De River bridge battle, senior South Vietnamese military and political leaders deeply appreciated what Lippard, his fellow Marines and the Navy had done. Lippard was quickly summoned to an ARVN headquarters and awarded the Vietnamese Cross of Gallantry with Palm insignia, the first of three he earned. Later, Vietnam's then-Premier, Nguyen Cao Ky, recognized Lippard for his distinguished actions in defending the bridge.

Why top U.S. officers never acknowledged Corporal Lippard's role in the Ca De River bridge battle and decimation of a large enemy force in late July 1965 remains a glaring unknown. Theories abound, and there are probably bits of truth in each. Marine commanders, at that time, were convinced their communication links had been compromised. Reporting through regular channels that a major headquarters and the vital Da Nang airbase came within a whisker of being overrun and wiped out by a Viet Cong force augmented by Communist (dubbed "Red" by Marines) Chinese soldiers might have alerted North Vietnamese interceptors that U.S. and ARVN forces were spread dangerously thin south of the Ca De River. Such knowledge certainly would have emboldened VC commanders to try taking the bridge again. As it was, a few days later, on 5 August, Viet Cong troops managed to blow up fuel tanks containing about 2,000,000 gallons of jet fuel near Da Nang.

Or maybe acknowledging that a solitary U.S. Marine was outside the allowed operating area—north of the bridge, in ARVN territory—and calling in U.S. Navy gunfire to wipe out a large enemy force was considered too sensitive for political palates. At the time, South Vietnamese military leaders were suspicious of U.S. intentions and quick to call foul.

Had the VC 7th Battalion broken through and destroyed critical strike aircraft and helicopters on the Da Nang air base flight line in late July, a key Marine attack at Chu Lai, planned for mid-August, might have been scrubbed. Nobody in the U.S. chain of command dared admit that the Marine Corps came very close to suffering one of its worst defeats in history, just as that major offensive was in the offing. Especially at a politically sensitive time, when the White House and Pentagon desperately needed a victory to establish U.S. credibility in Vietnam.

Ironically, 614 Viet Cong were killed and nine taken prisoner in the subsequent Chu Lai battle—about the same as North Vietnam lost in one night at the Ca De River bridge. And 45 Marines were killed and 120 wounded in the week-long battle at Chu Lai. In contrast, none were lost, during a furious, five-hour shootout north of the Ca De River that night of 28-29 July.

For whatever reason, the 18-24 August 1965 battle at Chu Lai is hailed as the U.S.'s "decisive first victory" by historians, while a deadly storm of fire and steel that erased an entire Viet Cong battalion almost one month earlier is never mentioned in official and scholarly accounts of the Vietnam War. At least none have surfaced. Was it buried in official secrecy born of near-miss embarrassment? Or intentionally "overlooked" and conveniently forgotten?

For his extraordinary central role in holding a crucial river crossing, Lippard never received a blip of public acknowledgment, word of high-rank congratulations or simple "thanks"—let alone a medal—from his own country. Not even a purple heart for a wound received in heavy combat that night.

True to Karl Lippard form, though, he doesn't really care. Instead, he chooses to emphasize that the Ca De River battle is a testament to the historically effective American military philosophy of training its warriors to improvise on the fly and do what it takes to get the job done. The savage fight of 28-29 July 1965 is also a loud-and-clear example of the trust placed in every Marine "Raider", whose call for artillery, air or naval gunfire support isn't questioned. Those holding the lightning bolts of American power merely "Roger" and commence firing or dropping on targets the Marine designates.

In Lippard's four-year tour as an active-duty Marine, he was wounded seven times and finally returned to the states on a gurney. He was offered a field commission to 2nd Lieutenant, but declined. Instead, he was promoted to Sergeant (E-5) and assigned to the drill field, turning fresh recruits into a new generation of Marines. Thanks to right-shoulder wounds, Lippard had the distinction of being the only Marine permitted to salute with his left hand.

He worked in the aerospace, property development and construction sectors for several years, but ultimately established himself as a world-class gun maker and designer. He holds 23 pistol patents, has another 147 pending, and is a vocal advocate for re-arming America's military forces and

Corporal Karl Lippard (left) and Lance Corporal Arturo Nunez, one of Lippard's machine gun team members.

citizens, following decades of incessant assaults that drove most U.S. firearms and ammunition manufacturers out of business.

Today, Karl Lippard is committed to reversing that trend and ensuring the United States can defend itself against all enemies, all the time. His vision covers the spectrum from semiautomatic .45-caliber pistols and unique rifles (his patented designs) to a new class of naval Gunship Destroyers capable of once again supporting troops ashore. He currently holds a $65-billion letter-of-commitment that underwrites a proposal to build and deliver 50 of these cutting-edge gunships for the U.S. Navy.

But that's another story in the Karl Lippard saga. After seven decades, this seasoned, scarred American warrior is still fighting and winning.

WARRIORS DENIED

After his account was first published in 2018, Karl Lippard's incredible story rapidly circulated among retired Marine and Navy communities via the magic of Internet. Soon, hundreds of Vietnam veterans separated by half a century were networking and reconnecting. Many who had been aboard the two destroyers—USS Craig and USS Stoddard—vividly recalled their response to a Marine Raider's Mayday call and collectively firing more than 400 five-inch rounds to destroy a large enemy force near Da Nang in the summer of 1965.

When Lippard was invited to address a reunion of USS Stoddard sailors in San Pedro, California, critical tidbits of information, ranging from personal tales to vital strategic data, began to surface. For example, Karl later received a call from a veteran, who said, "I was the radarman on the other end of your comm link that night. We thought you'd been killed!" In fact, most of Stoddard's sailors were unaware that an entire Viet Cong battalion had been decimated by their ship's and the USS Craig's sustained shelling.

A subsequent e-mail message from a former Stoddard sailor capsulized sentiments of those attending that September 2018 reunion:

"*During my 11 months in Vietnam, many involved in [Naval Gunfire Support], every mission was important. However, a few, including the Ca De River Bridge and the Esso Storage Tank missions, stand out as being more intense and critical. Karl, we were aware there was a 'group of Marines' in a dire situation, when ordered to the area. I think I speak for the entire crew of the [USS] Stoddard when I say, it wasn't until your presentation and e-mails that we realized just how dire the situation actually was. I'm unable to find the words to describe exactly how awestruck we are to have been able to participate in such a critical mission. ...[We] are extremely proud to have been a part in this intense battle, very gratified to have learned that not a single Marine was lost, and we thank you and your entire platoon for your bravery and service.*"

Information Karl acquired at the reunion—augmented by bits and pieces either e-mailed to him or that he and this writer located—started answering decades-old questions. Documents that Karl never knew existed were unearthed in TheVietnam Center and Sam Johnson Vietnam Archive at Texas Tech University. These included Marine situation reports, ship gunfire records and regimental documents. Even handwritten notes jotted down by a ship's historian, backed by photos taken from the USS Craig, before it departed Da Nang harbor on 29 July, helped validate two conclusions: 1) An intense, five-hour battle took place north of the Ca De River bridge on the night of 28-29 July 1965; and 2) that strategically critical battle was covered up—intentionally.

The latter assertion is backed by official records, as well as clumsy attempts—now glaringly obvious—to obscure or rewrite history. For example, dates were altered and misinformation inserted in routine operational reports. Key sentences in Navy and Marine Corps battle records were redacted for no logical reason. In fact, a six-line report of action on 29 July 1965 was 100 percent redacted. Totally blacked-out.

Powerful somebodies at 3rd Marine Division and Pacific Fleet headquarters apparently decided to purge all evidence of a critical battle that had occurred near the Ca De River bridge the night of 28-29 July. Staffers hid what they could and redacted what could not be altered or buried.

A diligent historian perusing sparse Navy and USMC records from

Gearing-class destroyer firing five-inch guns from forward mount
Bill Latta

that period would be baffled by conflicting reports about combat actions, mixed-up dates and "frag orders" that make little sense. Still, undeniable facts and gems of reliable information are there, if one knows where to look for specifics. In Lippard's terse terms, "It takes someone who was there and knows what really happened."

Certain irrefutable records were either overlooked or proved too difficult to alter. For example, ships' naval gunfire support documents identify precise coordinates crews fired upon the night of 28-29 July 1965. These long strings of numbers match those that Karl Lippard called out and later recorded, expecting to be debriefed by his superiors.

Division records also clearly note that the USS Craig was ordered to Da Nang Bay at max speed the night of 28 July to support Marines under attack. Its officers were told to contact a Marine spotter on a specific, rarely used radio frequency. Terminology used in these records banish any doubts that Division officers (specifically Major General Walt) were acutely aware of the critical situation unfolding at the bridge, and that failure to defeat the 7th VC battalion there would have devastating impacts.

But what justified taking extreme measures to literally "disappear" a major engagement, the first significant U.S. battle of the Vietnam War, a battle that should be proudly recorded in Navy and Marine Corps histories? That question has motivated retired officers and enlisted personnel to search for answers. Many queried Pentagon contacts and petitioned archive offices.

This writer and other former military officers sent the original Steel Storm story and a letter to President Donald Trump, requesting his assistance in securing well-deserved decorations for then-Corporal Lippard and the USS Craig and USS Stoddard crews. A typical response—on White House stationery—assured that "your correspondence [has been] forwarded to the appropriate federal agency for further action."

Three months hence, a letter from J. E. Nierle, president of the Navy Department Board of Decorations and Medals, asserted that "we are currently gathering information," and conducting "a review of Mr. Lippard's service record."

Another seven months passed, before similar rejection letters were sent to all petitioners. Speaking for the Navy board president, Mr. B. Hennen expressed regret that "no action can be taken on your request," because bureaucrats could find "no evidence to suggest Mr. Lippard has ever been nominated for a personal decoration" related to combat actions at the Ca De River bridge. Because decades have passed, a nomination now must be "submitted by an officer with standing via a Member of Congress." An enclosed pamphlet detailed stringent requirements, such as:

- A nominating officer must have been in Karl Lippard's "chain of command, or had firsthand knowledge of the heroic act, or meritorious service…"
- And that officer "was senior to [Lippard] in either grade or position at the time of the act."

Originators of a recommendation package "bear the burden of conducting all necessary research to gather supporting evidence," such as obtaining eyewitness statements and endorsements by Lippard's commanding officer and "all other surviving members of the original chain of command."

After more than half a century, only one such officer is known to be alive, and absolutely no American "eyewitnesses" ever existed, because Karl Lippard was the sole U.S. combatant engaged in the fight ashore. Technically, crews of both ships were eyewitnesses, but the night was pitch dark and it was raining. None of the crewmembers laid eyes on the Marine spotter directing their fire. In short, precise requirements dictated by today's Washington desk jockeys are impossible to satisfy.

Meanwhile, Karl Lippard was diligently trying to obtain a relatively low-level—yet treasured—Combat Action Ribbon (CAR) for the USS Craig and USS Stoddard. He assembled and delivered several packages of supporting data and records, but these were returned intact. One wonders whether they were ever opened, let alone reviewed.

Lippard also received several letters from B. Hennen, Executive Secretary of the Navy Board of Decorations and Medals, assuring that its staff had "reviewed all pertinent official records available…. Unfortunately, the evidence does not substantiate an award of the CAR to either ship."

Incredibly, Hennen claimed that official "records related to the actions of USS JOHN R. CRAIG or USS STODDARD on July 28-29 1965, indicate those ships were part of pre-planned naval gunfire support missions, and that neither vessel was under enemy fire. …We must presume the Navy had access to the official operations reports of the incident, and based on those, determined the ships did not meet the CAR criteria."

Absolutely false. The USS Craig was dispatched to the Ca De River bridge area by Major General Walt in response to Karl Lippard's Mayday plea. The ship pulled anchor and sailed immediately, leaving the ship's captain ashore. The Stoddard appeared several hours later, jumped into the violent battle and helped the Craig obliterate the 7th VC, which was desperately attempting to capture the bridge. The claim that this was a "pre-planned naval gunfire support mission" or minor exercise—what Lippard calls "sky busting"—is laughable.

Photo taken from the USS Craig after exiting Da Nang Bay in the early morning of 29 July 1965 shows smoke over the battlefield pounded by 443 five-inch rounds. An Esso oil storage complex barely visible in the center was blown up by Viet Cong sappers on 5 August, a week after the Ca De River Bridge battle.

Navy EM3 Hank Lehtola

Further, both ships' crews recall small arms rounds hitting their ships, fired by enemy soldiers shooting at Lippard, South Vietnamese Ranger Sgt. Thi and two destroyers delivering death in a violent storm of five-inch shells. When a Viet Cong mortar round exploded in the water between Lippard (on the shore) and the ships, both firing all their five-inch guns broadside, the Stoddard shifted to a position farther from the beach. There's no question that both vessels were under enemy fire. So, why were records altered to eliminate that factoid?

Finally, this writer's research yielded what may be the overriding reasons for intentionally covering up the ferocious Ca De River bridge fight that destroyed an entire enemy battalion: Protecting the president and keeping China out of the war. In his bestselling book, *Dereliction of Duty* (pp. 321-322), H.R. McMaster reports that, on 28 July 1965, President Lyndon B. Johnson "left the Pentagon for the news conference…. Just after 12:30 [p.m.], when the television audience would be the smallest, [LBJ] walked into the East Room of the White House" to give reporters an update on troop buildups in Vietnam. During that briefing, "…Johnson again denied that forces deployed to Vietnam were already engaged in combat operations."

Karl Lippard's heroic defense of the Ca De River bridge, backed by two destroyers, occurred on that same date, 28 July 1965. Given that Vietnam is on the other side of the International Date Line, the engagement may have already occurred. Whether Johnson knew about the massive shootout is unclear. Nevertheless, his aides and every military officer between Corporal Lippard and the White House weren't about to suggest the president had either lied or "misspoke." To avoid White House embarrassment, the battle would simply have to disappear—be erased from history, as if it had never happened.

Senior Navy and Marine Corps officers evidently chose to not report that a solitary Marine Raider had called in more than 400 rounds of Navy five-inch rounds to annihilate a 600-man unit of Viet Cong and Chinese regulars, thereby proving the commander-in-chief had misled the American people. Although historians now agree that LBJ and his Secretary of Defense, Robert McNamara, routinely lied to U.S. citizens, today's Deep State bureaucrats may still be protecting a favored president's legacy to preclude yet another blemish.

That said, senior players in the chain-of-command may have had legitimate concerns that they thought warranted burying this historic battle. The president and Defense chief McNamara lived in constant fear that Communist China would jump into the Vietnam War, threatening a Korean War redux or igniting World War III. If the news media exposed the fact that Chinese soldiers were fighting alongside Viet Cong and North Vietnamese troops, and roughly 300 uniformed regulars had died at the hands of U.S. Marine and Navy forces, might China feel compelled to respond?

Obviously, China's generals knew the People's Liberation Army had lost hundreds of its crack troops at the Ca De River bridge. But unless America or China openly acknowledged that fact, both sides could pretend it never happened. Consequently, keeping the media and American people in the dark might have seemed the best political solution.

The fear-of-China theory is underscored by another strange "operation" that took place shortly after the Ca De River bridge shootout. A Navy explosive ordnance disposal (EOD) team supposedly was dispatched to the precise area bombarded by the Craig and Stoddard in response to Karl Lippard's directives. Ostensibly, the team's mission was to "disable unexploded ordnance." Conflicting records indicate it either made a quick in-and-out excursion, or spent an unusual amount of time scouring that hellish killing ground. Did a team of EOD specialists remove every scrap of paper, insignia, clothing and personal items that could prove hundreds of Chinese soldiers had died there?

Reliable records of such a team's activities in that area have yet to surface—if they exist at all. In fact, Lippard tracked down the first EOD specialist deployed to Vietnam. Mr. EOD confirmed that he never set foot in-country until late 1965, months after the Ca De River battle. If not an EOD team, then who cleaned up the battlefield? On whose orders?

A half-century has passed, since Karl Lippard survived that horrific battle north of the Ca De River bridge. Despite his yeoman efforts, the two ships that answered his call probably will never receive a Combat Action Ribbon for their unquestioned support of a Marine in dire straits. And, unless a president of the United States personally sees fit to honor him, Karl Lippard will never receive well-deserved awards for his heroism under enemy fire.

As he's stated time and again, Karl is less concerned with personal decorations than he is about ensuring the bravery and professionalism exhibited by Craig and Stoddard crews are recognized. How those men performed in the Ca De River bridge battle is a testament to the long tradition of sailors supporting Marines under attack, delivering immediate, accurate, withering fire from offshore. Nevertheless, Navy Department Board of Decorations and Medals bureaucrats have deemed the matter closed. In short, they firmly ordered, "Don't bother us again."

Perhaps records of that ferocious fight on 28-29 July 1965 were altered, redacted and "disappeared" to protect a president and assuage worries about China's potential response. But President Johnson and China's hard-nosed leaders of the 1960s are long gone.

Nearly six decades later, it's time to correct manipulated, distorted records and honor the warriors who saved America's vaunted Marine Corps from a devastating defeat in mid-1965. Had the 7th VC battalion batted aside Lippard and a small cadre of Marines guarding the Ca De River bridge, the Vietnam War would have unfolded much differently. Exactly how will be left for true historians to speculate.

Lippard may not care about personal commendations, but the President of the United States, Secretary of the Navy, Commandant of the Marine Corps, and Chief of Naval Operations damn sure should. If future generations of Marines and sailors aren't taught their hallowed history, salted with stories of uncommon valor and performance of duty under fire, how will they learn and truly understand the meaning of "Honor"?

America must acknowledge and honor the unselfish actions of its warriors. It's the solemn duty of a grateful nation. If America fails to recognize and tangibly express appreciation for sacrifices made by her warriors—the men and women who fought and lived or died for their country—will future generations answer their nation's call to give their lives in the name of liberty? Maybe not.

> *"The willingness with which our young people are likely to serve in any war, no matter how justified, shall be directly proportional to how they perceive the veterans of earlier wars were treated and appreciated by their nation."*
>
> George Washington

Sergeant Karl Lippard as a drill instructor at Marine Corps Recruit Depot, San Diego, CA

Based on the few official records available, and the memories of those involved in the Ca De River bridge engagement of 28-29 July 1965. Photos and graphics courtesy of Karl Lippard and ship websites.

William B. Scott is the former Rocky Mountain Bureau Chief for Aviation Week & Space Technology magazine, author of The Permit, a techno-thriller novel, and coauthor of License to Kill: The Murder of Erik Scott; Space Wars: The First Six Hours of World War III; Counterspace: The Next Hours of World War III, and Inside the Stealth Bomber: The B-2 Story. As a commercial pilot with instrument and multi-engine ratings, and a Flight Test Engineer graduate of the U.S. Air Force Test Pilot School, he has logged approximately 2,000 flight hours on 81 types of aircraft. He holds a Bachelor of Science degree in Electrical Engineering.

AW SHIT SHACK!
"Farmer"

My first combat mission over North Vietnam would be a hard-hitting, eight-bomb strike against a major vehicle-repair facility in Hanoi. We were going Downtown.

As the new-guy pilot, I was assigned the Number Two position in a four-ship formation, our flight leader's right wingman. My back-seater or guy-in-back (GIB) was Rooster, an experienced F-4D Phantom Weapon Systems Officer, who had logged several missions over the North.

Phantom flight headed for North Vietnam
U.S. Air Force

Preflight was routine. While Rooster was firing up our bird's Inertial Navigation System, I conducted the walkaround, confirming all bits and pieces of the mean-looking, camouflage-green fighter were in the right places and firmly secured. The F-4D was configured with two AIM-7 radar-guided air-to-air missiles, two Electronic Countermeasures or ECM pods, a couple of 370-gallon wing tanks filled with JP-4 fuel, and a pair of massive 2,000-pound Laser Guided Bombs (LGB). To confuse radar-guided surface-to-air missiles (SAM), bundles of chaff—strips of aluminum foil—were tucked inside the F-4D's speed brakes.

Takeoff, join up and the flight up north were uneventful. We rendezvoused with a KC-135 tanker and took turns topping off our fuel tanks, before crossing into North Vietnam. With ECM pods beeping and squeaking, our semi-spread formation of four jets created an indistinct blob of noise on enemy radars. To avoid a SAM fused to detonate at a predetermined altitude in the middle of that blob, our four-ship repeatedly drifted down a few hundred feet, then climbed back up to roughly 18,000 ft.

As we approached Hanoi, Lead wagged his wings, signaling us to maneuver into a fingertip formation. The mission called for a pull-up, then 90-degree roll-in delivery, which meant the flight would bank steeply at the initial point, roll into a 45-deg. dive, and when altitude, airspeed and dive angle parameters came together, Lead would call, "Pickle!" Each pilot would mash a button on the control stick, releasing two 2,000-pound LGBs.

Meanwhile, Lead's GIB would be firing a laser beam from a Pave Knife pod mounted near his F-4D's wing root. When locked on the target, reflected laser light would create a cone or "basket" with its vertex on that vehicle repair joint. Because this was long before the days of automatic tracking, the GIB used a small TV screen and hand controller to manually hold the Pave Knife's laser crosshairs on our target. Not easy, but if he successfully lased the repair facility throughout our delivery and about six seconds of laser-guided free-fall, eight 2,000-pounders would obliterate the target.

Eyes glued to Lead's wingtip, my heart rate ratcheted up a few notches as the four-ship rolled in and started downhill. Weapons selected. Master Arm switch on. Speed brakes out… NOW! Our chaff bundles scattered in unison, creating a huge cloud of tin foil and, hopefully, hiding four Phantoms from the bad guys' deadly radar-guided surface-to-air missiles.

Thumb poised over the weapon-release button, we dived smartly, airspeed retarded a bit by those big slabs of speed brakes. Radio calls from all over North Vietnam assaulted my helmet-covered ears, which strained to hear Lead's call through the nonstop cacophony of SAM-generated warning tones and transmitted warnings:

"SAMs! Four o'clock!"

"Break right! MiGs on your tail!"

"Break left! Hard LEFT!"

Confusion reigned, overwhelming the mission frequency with frantic radio calls, squeals, static, beeps from emergency beacons and scrambled babble. Over the noise, I heard it: "Pickle! Pickle! Pickle!"

I jammed the weapons release button and felt our hulking fighter thump as 4,000 pounds of steel, high explosives and expensive laser-guidance kits departed.

Bombs away! ...Aw shit!

Lead's bombs were still snugged up under his wings, as he and the other two Phantoms continued a steep dive. Heartbeats later, I heard his distinctive call, "Pickle! Pickle! Pickle!" A shower of LGBs fell away from three F-4s. But not mine. I'd already launched my pair of 2,000-pound blivets. To where, I had no idea.

Lead started a gentle straight-ahead pull-up, while his GIB carefully tracked our target, holding the Pave Knife crosshairs over those six LGBs' final destination. We flew directly over the target, roughly 10,000 feet above the impending firestorm and outside anti-aircraft gun range. Lead banked and wagged his rudder, signaling us to maneuver back into a spread formation.

Exiting the target area's threats of flak and missiles, I struggled to keep up with the formation. Throttles full forward in military power, I kept falling back, lagging the other aircraft. What the....? Had we been hit? All cockpit gauges confirmed critical systems were humming and happy. Both General Electric J-79 engines were faithfully producing up to 17,000 lb. of thrust. To hang onto Lead's wing, though, I had to select both afterburners, consuming precious fuel at a scary rate. It felt like we were dragging an 18-wheeler truck!

Frantically, I kept scanning the instrument panel, mind racing. *What's wrong, old girl?*

A brain flash of No-way; you-gotta-be-shittin'-me: I'd left the speed brakes out, as we pulled up, following the bomb-delivery maneuver! Functioning exactly as designed, those flat-plate boards sticking into the airstream were creating beaucoup drag, battling against the J-79s' thrust. And, of course, devouring our fuel.

Then our Number Four called, "MiG at six! Firing missiles!" Lead commanded a hard right break-turn to evade missiles trying to lock onto an unlucky F-4. Back into afterburner. Even more precious fuel gulped and gobbled. Number Two was rapidly sinking into deep-kimchi trouble.

"Four" finally called an all-clear. The enemy missiles were tumbling out of control and that MiG had vanished.

Rooster and I did some quick fuel calculations and concluded we wouldn't make it back to base. I'd screwed up big time. Nothing to do but call Lead and confess that our skosh fuel situation had put us in hurt-city.

Fortunately, a gutsy KC-135 tanker crew crossed the Laos-North Vietnam border, enabling me to link up and take on a few thousand pounds of life-giving JP-4 with only minutes to spare. As my heart rate slowed to something approaching normal, I swore undying allegiance to every tanker driver in the U.S. Air Force.

Back in formation, our four-ship flew home with no further excitement. However, I'd never felt lower. First combat mission and I'd blown it. Years of hard work—ROTC in college, pilot training, Phantom transition, air-to-air and air-to-ground training, and finally realizing a long-held dream, flying fighters…. All down the proverbial tube! When it came time to put everything on the line in combat, I'd messed up royally. Probably be grounded. Maybe sent back to the states, banished to a training squadron, flying Cessna T-37 "Tweets" for the rest of a brief, boring career. *Damn!*

F-4 Phantom, post-landing, drag chute deployed
U.S. Air Force Photo

After landing, taxi and shutdown, I silently crammed a kneeboard, checklist, helmet and oxygen mask into an olive-drab bag. I'd just stepped off the ladder, when a colonel pulled up in a staff car. Glumly, I slinked over and started mumbling.

"I'm really sorry, sir. I screwed up. Thought I heard Lead call…"

"What the hell you talking about, Captain? What shape's your airplane in? Is it up for another mission?" the colonel barked. A maintenance officer!

Stunned, I stammered, "Uhh… Yes, sir! Code One, sir! No squawks. Good to go, sir."

Back at the squadron, our flight lead—a veteran fighter pilot—began the mission debriefing by asking a question I was dreading: "What happened to all your fuel?" I admitted leaving my speed brakes out, as we came off the target. I didn't mention the early pickle.

After a long pause, Lead simply growled, "I'll bet you won't do that again."

That was it. "Farmer" had lived to fly the Phantom another day! Somehow, some way, the God that watches over green fighter pilots had taken pity on this ol' country boy.

A few days later, I was scanning a newspaper, when a small article caught my eye. Evidently, Paris peace talks had been disrupted by indignant North Vietnamese accusations that American pilots had bombed a sensitive facility very important to the Communists. It was deep in Hanoi, not far from a major vehicle repair facility. American negotiators adamantly denied that the sacrosanct edifice had been targeted by U.S. forces.

I carefully reread the article, a big grin spreading across my young mug. Maybe, just maybe, Farmer's bombs hadn't been wasted.

Farmer went on to fly 200 combat missions, many over North Vietnam. A few years later, he was selected for USAF Test Pilot School and logged several thousand hours as both an Air Force and civilian test pilot. He retired as a full colonel from the Air Force Reserves, and recently from a major aerospace firm as its chief test pilot.

MIRACLE MISSION
William B. Scott

Exactly seven years, to the day, after graduating from pilot training, Major Richard (Dick) Benson saddled up for his 33rd combat sortie, a daytime Visual Reconnaissance (VR) mission over North Vietnam. A few feet behind him, Captain Gerald Dobberfuhl, an experienced reconnaissance officer, settled into the rear cockpit of their camera-equipped RF-4C Phantom fighter. The two had been mated as a crew, while transitioning to the RF-4C at Mountain Home AFB, Idaho, then shipped to Udorn AB in Thailand.

Dick Benson (fourth from left) and Gerry Dobberfuhl (left end) transitioned to the RF-4C Phantom in early 1969.

At the time, RF-4Cs were flying two types of reconnaissance missions. Dick preferred low-and-fast daytime VR. Because Gerry favored the night option and using the LORAN (Long Range Navigation) system to find targets, they compromised: Fly VR missions for three months, then request night LORAN recce.

Typically, RF-4C crews worked with F-4 "Fast FACs" (Forward Air Controllers) in eastern Laos, along the North Vietnam border, to locate and photograph targets. The FACs would then mark the area and call in bomb-laden fighters to hit the enemy. Risks were high, because VR and FAC F-4 crews often stayed in strike areas for hours, refueling several times from airborne tankers.

The 16 September 1969 mission was slated to revisit a well-defended area Benson and Dobberfuhl had photographed a few days earlier, working with an F-4 FAC. Their objective—a road hugging the side of a mountain pass along the North Vietnam-Laos border—subsequently was bombed by a four-ship flight of F-105 Thunderchief fighters. About 15 minutes after their bombing runs, Benson had made a low pass for post-strike photos, flying a northeast-to-southwest track from the North Vietnam side. The enemy was still manning their guns and opened up on the recce bird racing over a still-smoking target zone. Tracers sliced across the RF-4C's nose, but enemy gunners had led the fighter a bit too much and the Phantom returned intact. No bullet holes.

The same crew wouldn't be so lucky on 16 September.

To visually check repairs made to the mountain road bombed a few days earlier, Benson and Dobberfuhl dropped to tree-skimming altitude and set up for a fast pass from the Laotian side of the border. Dick rolled into a steep right bank and pulled his jet around the shoulder of a mountain, expecting to surprise ground troops.

Run in fast, eyeball the road and get out of Dodge, before the bad guys could react.

Banked 120-degrees, RF-4C No. 908 flashed across North Vietnamese anti-aircraft gunners, who unleashed a barrage of lead at the twin-engine, camouflage-green monster. Dobberfuhl heard a sharp explosion, as a single 12.7-millimeter round blasted a hole through the front-cockpit canopy.

"I'm hit!" Benson choked. A thumb-size slug had shattered a small compass mounted on his survival vest, obliterated the parachute harness's chest strap and plowed a fist-size hole in the pilot's torso. Ground crews later found a bullet embedded in the fighter's fuel-control panel, aft of the throttles.

"It felt like a mule had kicked me in the chest. I couldn't catch my breath," Benson recalled. Still in control, he rolled wings-level on a northeast heading—into North Vietnam—jammed twin throttles into afterburner and

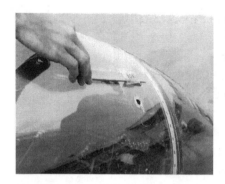

pulled up to a steep climb. "Gerry took control, not knowing what shape I was in. Passing through 10,000 feet, I pulled the throttles out of AB, hoping he would understand that the cockpits wouldn't pressurize with that hole in my canopy."

No way. Dobberfuhl jammed both throttles back into afterburner and kept them there. Despite burning JP-4 fuel at an enormous rate, the jet blasted through Mach 1 and headed for home supersonically. Gerry had taken flying lessons on his own time, but the 20-ton, twin-engine fighter was in a far different class than the general aviation bug-smashers he'd flown.

Slicing into clouds and disappearing from gunners' sights, Dobberfuhl had plenty to worry about. He had no idea how badly the Phantom was damaged. Were its fuel tanks hit? Could the jet explode at any second?

"My eyes turned to the escape handle," he later recounted in a Guideposts article. One pull and both he and Benson would be ejected from the crippled aircraft. But how badly was the pilot wounded?

A low groan from up-front made the decision. Ejecting Benson at supersonic speed almost certainly would kill him. Not an option.

Dobberfuhl concentrated on flying the big bird. A quick check of his flight chart showed the closest friendly airfield was Nakhon Phanom (NKP), about 70 miles away. Medical help would be available there. It was Benson's best chance for survival.

Get him on the ground ASAP!

Gerry held the throttles in afterburner, keeping the fighter in supersonic territory. But a host of fear-laced concerns crowded his brain.

How am I going to land this bird? he worried. Forward visibility from the RF-4C's rear cockpit was blocked by an instrument panel and electronic gear.

Downward views from the back seat were blocked by broad engine intakes along each side of the fuselage.

He'd worry about that later.

Dobberfuhl also mentally wrestled with how to extend the landing gear. The gear handle was in the forward cockpit. Yes, he could "blow" the gear down from the back, but it was an emergency measure that risked rupturing the utility hydraulic system and causing all sorts of havoc. Probably lose brakes and nose wheel steering. Not good.

Benson was in shock, but still conscious. "Although Gerry was a nav [navigator], I knew he'd done some private aircraft flying, and I often let him fly [the RF-4C] from the back," Dick said. "I was confident he could get us to NKP. I'm glad he stuck with the aircraft. Nobody would have criticized him, if he'd ejected. But I'm sure I wouldn't have made it, if he'd punched us out."

Approaching NKP, Dobberfuhl called the tower, declared an emergency and informed controllers he hoped to "take the barrier." Cables stretched across each end of the runway, suspended several inches off the tarmac by rubber standoffs, could be snagged by a fighter's extended tail hook. Gerry didn't know whether he'd have operational brakes, after landing, and taking the barrier would be a smart precaution. Except for one little problem. The Phantom's tail hook could only be lowered from the front cockpit.

He descended, following radio directives from a Ground Controlled Approach specialist. "Above glide slope. Descending. On glide slope. Come left five degrees," the controller droned, literally talking the crew down.

"Somewhere inside of 10 miles, I spotted the runway," Benson said. "But I was getting tunnel vision from loss of blood. When I felt we had the runway made, I told Gerry I had the field in sight, and lowered the gear, flaps and tail hook. I intended to make an approach-end barrier engagement."

Flying blind from the rear cockpit, making small adjustments as commanded by the GCA controller, Gerry was intensely focused on the approach. "Suddenly, like a ghost, Benson's voice came through [my helmet's] earphones. It startled me."

"I...I've got the field in sight," the pilot muttered, barely audible. A firm shake of the stick confirmed he had taken control. Landing and barrier engagement "went okay, and the barrier worked great," Benson recalled, the epitome of understatement.

Dick was fading in and out of consciousness, but managed to open his canopy. Dobberfuhl had to crawl forward on the left intake housing, reach into the front cockpit and shut down both engines. Dick recalls "about a dozen hands lifting me out of the cockpit" and being gently taken down a ladder. "I thought I had it made now."

A doctor in NKP's emergency room worked frantically to save Benson's life. Intravenous tubes were poked into both ankles. A one-inch incision just below the collarbone provided an opening for an instrument to deal with a collapsed lung. "I thought that was going to finish me off," Dick admitted.

Trying to stem blood flowing from the hole in his patient's chest, the physician dug out a small piece of bloodied silver. It was a Saint Christopher medal, a token worn to invoke the Catholic saint of protection. Bonnie Benson had given the medal to her husband, before he departed for Vietnam. Although neither was Catholic, "We didn't want to offend anyone for that year I was in combat," Dick smiles.

That Saint Christopher had been nicked by the 12.7-mm bullet, driving the silver medal into Dick's chest. Lying in the emergency room, Benson noticed a white-collared chaplain hovering nearby. Concerned that the padre might be there to administer last rites, Dick croaked, "I'm not Catholic, father."

"It wouldn't make any difference, son," the chaplain said softly.

Benson and Dobberfuhl were soon loaded onto a helicopter and flown to Udorn, their home base. When he woke up three days later, Dick was being shaved by an Air Force corpsman brandishing a straight razor. The pilot would log another 30 or so shaves, before leaving the Udorn hospital.

In Columbus, Ohio, Bonnie Benson and her two sons came home to find the dreaded Air Force blue staff car waiting for them. Fearing the worst and praying for the best, they were informed that Dick had been severely wounded, but was alive. Details were sketchy. His left lung had collapsed, a few ribs were chipped, and he had several holes in his intestines. Loss of skin and muscle eventually required a skin graft to close the massive chest wound.

Dick was hospitalized for six weeks, then flown home to recuperate. Credited with a completed combat tour, he was transferred to Hill AFB, Utah. He eventually returned to the cockpit as a test pilot, flying all models of the F-4, T-38 Talon and B-57 Canberra, before retiring in April 1976. He soon embarked on a second career as a corporate pilot, flying the Hawker 125 business jet for Thiokol Corporation.

Now retired a second time, Benson often reflects on the series of miracles that ensured he still walks the Earth: An enemy gunner's single round tore a massive hole in the pilot's chest, but narrowly missed the heart, because a Saint Christopher medal deflected the slug a hair. Maybe. A cool-headed backseater, who could fly a Phantom, made the tough decision to not eject. Staying conscious long enough to land safely. Having skilled military doctors, nurses and hospital technicians waiting in Thailand to put him back together. And a strong, loving wife back home, taking care of their family.

Speaking at a 445th Fighter Interceptor Squadron reunion, Richard E. Smith, a former prisoner of war who had endured five years of captivity in North Vietnam, honored the real heroes. "It didn't take heroic skills to get shot up or shot down," he said. The heroes were those who endured at home, being both mother and father to children, managing all family affairs, "while we were off doing our pilot thing."

Traumatic experiences leave indelible memories. "It's been over half a century," Dick says, "but that mission is as vivid today as it was in 1969. Yes, some details have faded with time. But I know, without a doubt: It was in the valley that I had one of my mountain top experiences."

Richard "Dick" Benson and William B. Scott with a Vietnam-era F-4 Phantom in the Hill AFB, Utah, air museum.
Linda G. Scott

SCRAMBLED EGGS—VIETNAM-STYLE

Major Tony Geishauser (US Army - Ret.)

It started as just another routine day at the office. Of course, my office happened to be the cockpit of a U.S. Army UH-1 "Huey" helicopter flying over Vietnam.

Every day started routinely. Some even ended that way. 16 March 1966, wouldn't be one of those days.

That morning, two 173rd Airborne Brigade cooks quickly loaded large containers of hot chow into our bird. Fully loaded and carrying a 400-lb. sling-load of ice, we headed for War Zone D north of Bien Hoa. Our LZ or Landing Zone was designated "Zulu-Zulu."

The 2nd Battalion of the 173rd had been in the field for several days, living on a diet of C-rations, and its airborne "Sky Soldiers" were badly in need of hot chow. My outfit—A Company, 82nd Aviation—carried troops to and from fire fights, provided medical-evacuation services and kept a steady resupply of ammo, "C-" and "A-rats," water, mail and, on rare occasions, ice to our ground-pounding brothers-in-arms. This morning, we were scheduled to deliver a hot breakfast and drink-cooling ice.

A few miles from our destination, we called the unit, asking it to pop a smoke grenade and identify the landing zone. I soon reported spotting red smoke. A radio operator responded, "Roger, red smoke, Cowboy. Wind calm. No Victor-Charlies in the AO." Good; a friendly Area of Operations. The Viet Cong were elsewhere this morning.

We made a slow pass over a hole in the jungle's canopy and decided our best approach was straight down into the LZ, some 100 feet below the treetops. The hole appeared big enough for us to hover through. Still, the crew chief and gunner stood on each of our helicopter's skids, talking us down and ensuring we didn't inadvertently back our tail rotor into a jagged tree line skirting the LZ. Without a tail rotor to compensate for the main rotor's torque, our Huey wouldn't hover; it'd spin and crash. So, keeping our tail out of those trees was a high priority.

We had just started down through the hole, when the jungle erupted. "Mack! Machine-gun tracers, two o'clock! Pull pitch, pull pitch!" I yelled.

Mack, the other pilot, saw what looked like basketball-size 0.51-caliber tracer rounds pass several yards in front of our chopper a second after I did. The enemy gunner, obviously trained to lead his target, expected us to fly into his line of fire. But we weren't flying forward. We were hovering straight down.

As Mack started to pull pitch, rotor RPM decayed. "Punch off the ice, Mack! Punch off the ice!" I yelled into my microphone. Mack didn't hear me, couldn't find the sling load release button on his stick or had a few other things on his mind. I didn't wait for an explanation. I kicked the manual release lever between my pedals and 400 pounds of ice fell away. Without that extra weight, rotor RPM slowly edged back into the green.

When Mack started easing us up through the treetops' opening, that enemy gunner swung his aim point, overcorrected and blasted our tail boom and tail rotor. The chopper started to spin, dropping toward the ground. I said what every helicopter pilot says at a time like this: *"Shit!"*

The closer we got to the ground, the faster my mind raced, which converted all activity into an illusion of slow motion. All the way down, I talked to myself: *I'm not going to get seriously killed.*

Heck, I even upped the ante. *I'm not even going to get hurt.* It worked—at least, the not-getting-killed part did. The foliage cushioned our fall somewhat, but the main rotor blades nearly shook the helicopter to pieces as they chopped trees into kindling.

Our Huey finally settled to the jungle floor, crashing on its left side with a final death heave.

Geishauser's UH-1 was shot down, while trying to deliver a hot breakfast to airborne troops. When the Huey arrived overhead, it was attacked by North Vietnamese regulars waiting in ambush.

Tony Geishauser

"Anyone hurt?" I shouted.

Everyone reported being OK, including the crew chief, whose back was nearly broken. Banged-up and bruised, we all scrambled out the right cargo door as fast as possible, slipping and sliding on broken eggs, orange juice and coffee.

I saw a figure running toward us, rifle in hand. Our gunner held his fire, identifying the man as a round-eyed airborne soldier. He'd been sent to escort us to safety.

As our last crew member scampered from the dead Huey, all hell broke loose. Hundreds upon hundreds of weapons started firing, all on full-automatic. The noise was deafening. The 700 or so men of the 2nd Battalion, 503rd Infantry were surrounded by a reinforced North Vietnamese Army (NVA) regiment of 2,000 regular soldiers, not ragtag Viet Cong rebels.

Once we were clear of the chopper, our 173rd paratrooper escort bent low to the ground and shouted that timeless infantry command: "Follow me!" We hauled for all we were worth, aiming for the center of the battalion's defensive position, perhaps 100 meters from where we had crashed.

We were directed to locations that might be out of harm's way, but those positions often changed as the battle raged. Two M-60 machine guns taken from our chopper helped shore up the battalion's defensive perimeter. A sergeant appeared, carrying our crew chief's now-broken M-14 rifle. Its wooden stock had snapped off during the crash landing, leaving only a trigger-housing group and hardware forward of it. The burly sergeant motioned for me to come closer, so I low-crawled over to him.

Stooped low, the paratrooper held the weapon below his waist and said, "When they break through, hold the trigger housing group here, in your groin. Grab the barrel and aim it with your left hand. There's not much kick when the M-14 fires. Don't worry about it. Just hit what you're shooting at and keep it on semiautomatic. Here are two more ammo clips. Any questions?"

Any questions? How did this day go from routine flying to John Wayne-style lessons about shooting bad guys with half a rifle, *when*—not *if*—they break through? I shook my head, which he took to mean "no questions." Actually, it was my way of saying, "Unbelievable; totally unbelievable."

The next four hours were a blur. Artillery, theirs and ours, fell inside and outside our perimeter. Fighter aircraft strafed us, because the enemy was literally right on top of our position. When I saw lead flying through the air, hitting two soldiers a few yards away, I thought Charlie had finally broken through. Surely, I would be the next to get it.

I made sure the ammo clip was firmly seated in the broken M-14 and a round was in the chamber. I waited.... But nothing happened. I finally realized the lead I'd seen must have been from a fighter strafing our zone. The perimeter hadn't been breached. The 2nd Bat was continuing to hold against overwhelming odds.

Box scores can't measure the strong hearts and brave souls of the men who comprised the 2nd Battalion, 503rd Infantry, 173rd Airborne Brigade, as they fought and defeated a fierce and determined enemy three times their number. After our sister battalion, the 1st of the 503rd, arrived—fighting through enemy lines to reinforce us—the body count was 11 Americans killed, 109 wounded. Later, we learned that more than 600 NVA bodies were found around the stubbornly held perimeter. There's no telling how many enemy wounded crawled away.

It had taken the 2nd Bat's sister battalion nearly four hours to hack its way through thick jungle to get to us. One of the men in that unit, Specialist Fourth Class Alfred Rascon, a medic, exercised "...extraordinary valor in the face of deadly enemy fire. His heroism in rescuing the wounded went well above and beyond the call of duty to protect and treat his wounded comrades…" as they fought their way to us, according to an award citation. For his heroic actions that non-routine day, he received the Congressional Medal of Honor.

When it came to flying helicopters, I knew what I was doing. But when it came to fierce in-your-face, gut-wrenching, close-quarters combat, there were no better soldiers than the 2nd Battalion, 503rd Infantry and its sister battalion, the 1st of the 503rd. Thanks, "Sky Soldiers," for saving a helicopter crew and my bacon on a day when we were simply trying to bring you eggs and bacon.

Fast-forward some 36 years. The 173rd Airborne Brigade was having a reunion in Fort Worth, TX. Not long before, I had linked-up with the 2nd Battalion's radio operator via the Internet. He invited me to come to the reunion and speak to his comrades. Very few of those soldiers had met the Huey pilot who'd crashed in the LZ, dumping their bacon and eggs that fateful day.

I did go to the reunion—right after stopping at a McDonald's public relations office. Concluding my 5-min. speech to the reunion's ex-soldiers, I said, "The 'Cowboys' always deliver, even if it takes a second try, thirty-some years later." To a standing ovation, I handed out more than 300 McDonald's Egg McMuffin gift certificates.

Tony Geishauser (right) completed a full 20-year Army career, retiring as a major and a Master Army Aviator. In addition to being an infantry officer and helicopter pilot, he served as an Army public information officer in Europe and at the world's largest military post, Fort Hood, Texas. He later held positions as a worldwide media relations and advertising manager for Texas Instruments, and media relations positions at other companies for more than 19 years.

NIGHT BOMBER: THE B-57G
Ad Thompson

B-57G Canberra
Martin Marietta

FIRST JETS TO VIETNAM

In the early 1960s, the US government was gravely concerned about communist aggression in Southeast Asia, specifically in Vietnam. U.S. advisors were assisting the military forces of South Vietnam (SVN), but after the Tonkin Gulf incident in late 1964, America's involvement escalated quickly. A mad scramble to send U.S. jet aircraft to SVN and bolster the South Vietnamese air force also served to expand U.S. combat operations.

The first U.S. jet to initially see combat was the Martin B-57 Canberra. Two squadrons of B-57Bs stationed in Japan (with a nuclear mission) were moved to Clark Air Base in the Phillipines and converted to a conventional role. A few days after the Tonkin Gulf incident, the 13th Squadron was ordered to Bien Hoa, SVN. At first, the aircraft were merely a show of force, flying reconnaissance and courier missions. However, they suffered considerable damage from VC attacks on the base. Finally, in early 1965, the 8th and 13 th were cleared to begin offensive operations.

TAKE BACK THE NIGHT

Many effective daytime ground attack missions were conducted by

8th and 13th air crews. However, the U.S. needed a capability to prevent North Vietnamese regulars and Viet Cong guerillas from moving troops and supplies at night and during bad weather. Consequently, several new projects were soon underway, developing high-tech systems to "take back the night." One of the more promising was Project Tropic Moon.

A pod fitted with Low Light Level Television (LLLTV) and laser range-finder, Tropic Moon initially was carried under the wings of four A-1E Skyraiders. Encouraging results led to a Tropic Moon II project, with units mounted on the wings of three B-57Bs. These projects demonstrated a potential for single-aircraft, armed reconnaissance at night. A decision was made to convert a full squadron of B-57s to a new model, the B-57G. This variant incorporated the LLLTV and laser rangefinder taken from Tropic Moon systems, as well as a new Forward Looking Infrared (FLIR) and forward-looking radar with a moving target indicator (MTI) feature. Sixteen B-57s were pulled from service and sent to Martin Marietta in Baltimore, Maryland, for modification. Meanwhile, other B-57B, C and E models also were being converted for duty in South Vietnam to replace combat losses and the sixteen jets being modified to G-models.

The 13th Squadron was deactivated in SVN, due to losses, and reestablished at MacDill AFB, Florida. The unit started flying the new B-57 G, equipped with FLIR, LLLTV, MTI radar and laser systems mounted under a new, bulbous nose radome. G-models also included state-of-the-art ejec-

tion seats, foam-filled fuel tanks and additional armor plating around the cockpit. None of these modifications improved the look, gross weight or aerodynamics, and greatly reduced the B-57's range, due to increased weight and drag.

One of the more innovative mods was a dispenser installed in the weapons bay. This modular unit resembled a huge egg crate with 21 square holes containing 21 cases of bomblets. Intended to be the primary weapon for interdicting operations on the Ho Chi Minh Trail, it proved to be of little use and was soon abandoned.

Because the B-57 community was somewhat inbred, "you couldn't go unless you'd already been." Consequently, most of the 13th Squadron pilots were majors and lieutenant colonels, many with previous combat experience in the B-57. I joined the newly reestablished 13th as one of only two pilots with the rank of captain. Soon after I checked out in the B-57G, I was made an instructor pilot and sent TDY to the Tactical Air Warfare Center at Eglin AFB, Florida, to conduct operational testing of the modified jet and its sensor systems.

Not long before the squadron moved to Southeast Asia, someone wondered if Tropic Moon's laser range finder had the correct frequency and signal strength to serve as a target illuminator for newly developed Paveway Laser-Guided bombs (LGB). If it did, a single jet could carry both bombs and the target illuminator. So, several of us flew over sensors designed to detect our lasers. Successful results from that one-night test mission set in motion plans for a new and better weapon system.

After the jets were tested at Eglin AFB—and completion of a lot of planning, training and additional testing by the "new" 13th Squadron—we launched a two-week, island-hopping journey across the Pacific to Ubon Royal Thai Air Base, Thailand. Now assigned to the USAF Tactical Air Command's (TAC) 8th Fighter Wing, we reinstalled equipment that had been removed for the ferry flights and began combat operations.

The first sorties were flown in daylight, familiarizing us with the terrain over which we would be operating at night. We flew the entire length of Eastern Laos, from the Plain of Jars in the north to Pakse in the south. No one fired at us, during daytime flights, but that changed, as we started night missions. Soon, being shot at by 23-mm, 37-mm, 57-mm, and larger-caliber guns became routine.

Veterans of earlier B-57B missions in South Vietnam flew the first night combat sorties, carrying the modular dispenser. Thanks to a poor bomblet dispersal pattern, seven of the system's 21 containers had to be delivered on each pass to have a reasonable probability of hitting a targeted truck. Even with a solid hit, bomblets generally didn't cause sufficient damage to destroy the truck. Consequently, those dispensers were removed from all the jets and replaced by the tried-and-true M-36 "Funny Bomb," which had proven to be the most successful truck-killer. Developed to ignite fires in Japan, this World War II weapon was a canister-type bomb similar

Funny Bomb in B-57G weapons bay
U.S. Air Fore

to Cluster Bomb Unit (CBU) ordnance. Nicknamed "funny bombs," the 900-pound M-36 was a combination of incendiary devices and CBUs—182 thermite bomblets that burned so intenesely one might believe they could ignite dirt. A single bomblet could set a truck afire and destroy it.

The downside for night operations was the bomblets' brilliant white blaze lasted 20-30 minutes, destroying our night vision and overloading the aircraft's sensors. To avoid these issues, I would drop on a suspected target, and, if there were no secondary explosions of ammunition or POL, look for other targets. Later, we'd return to count burning or burned-out hulks.

Since the B-57G operated as a single-ship, and all ordnance dropped in Laos had to be controlled by a forward air controller (FAC), all 13th pilots also were certified to serve as our own FACs.

A USAF & NAVY COMBAT FIRE-POWER DEMONSTRATION

For mission-planning purposes, Laos was divided into several geographic work areas to prevent interference. Our missions were fragged to a specific area, ensuring we were the only bird working that zone. One night, a Navy aircraft requested clearance into my work area to strike a target its crew had spotted on moving target indicator (MTI) radar. The Navy A-6 had an excellent MTI radar—much better than the B-57G's. We hadn't spotted any targets, so I got out of his way and cleared him in hot.

Because Navy crews were banned from taking ordnance back to the boat, the A-6 pilot said he'd salvo his entire load. I asked what he was carrying. He calmly reported having 24 Mk 82s (500-pound bombs) and four Rockeyes (500-pound armor-piercing cluster bombs).

Whoa! "Wait until I get back over there," I radioed. "I want to see this!" He did, and it was like watching a mini-B-52 bomber strike—a storm of violent explosions. He thanked me for the target and prepared to depart. Since I was close to bingo fuel and hadn't seen anything worth hitting, I told the Navy jock I was going to drop my bombs on his target.

"What do you have on board?" he asked.

"Four funny bombs." He immediately asked me to hold up, so he could swing back and watch. That was the only time I dropped four funny bombs at the same time. It was spectacular! And it definitely impressed our Navy brethren.

NEW BOMBS FOR AN OLD JET

The laser range-finder testing we had done at MacDill started paying off, when new laser-guided Mk 82 bombs started arriving. I much preferred these to the M-36s, because the 500-pounders exploded with no residual thermite fires to destroy night vision. Our sensors also enabled adjusting aim-point crosshairs, while a guided bomb was inflight.

The new system was optimized for level, ballistic deliveries from 3,000-5,000 feet. Our sensors weren't gimbaled beyond 90 degrees—looking straight down—but the LGBs required keeping our laser focused on the target, until impact. This meant the bomb often exploded well behind the jet. I found that starting a shallow dive, after bomb release, enabled holding crosshairs on-target until impact. Soon, we were successfully nailing convoys by dropping an LGB on the lead truck, then using M-36s to finish off the others.

A CIVILIAN FLYING A COMBAT MISSION

As previously mentioned, the MTI radar on our B-57s never performed as well in Vietnam as it did during testing in the U.S. The integrated system's radar was supposed to detect a moving target at sufficient range to get crosshairs on it, use the LLLTV or FLIR to refine the aim point and deliver the weapon. It never worked very well, despite tweaking at the manufacturer's factory and in our avionics shop. Finally, a Texas Instruments technical representative showed up at Ubon with orders to fly a combat mission and figure out why the radar didn't work in the field.

I was selected to fly the experienced tech rep, probably because I was the most junior instructor pilot (IP) in the squadron. Amazed that a civilian was authorized to fly on an actual combat mission, I briefed him thoroughly, emphasizing what to do, if we didn't make it back to base. Luckily, the mission concluded without incident and the rep took his data back to the factory. All to no avail. The radar never did work.

AWARDS "CEREMONY" IN A COMBAT ZONE

After about a month of flying combat missions, my roommate, Dave, and I were in our room, resting up for that night's mission. Joe M., our squadron's Awards and Decorations Officer, came into the room, carrying a stack of blue leather boxes under one arm. Wearing shorts, sandals and no shirt—standard squadron-area garb in Ubon's hot, humid climate—Joe asked if we had received our Air Medals yet. No, we hadn't. He casually tossed one to Dave and a second to me. "Here's yours and here's yours. Congratulations."

Then he was off to conduct an equally memorable ceremony for another crew. Typical for our squadron. In sharp contrast, a general officer awarded my final Distinguished Flying Cross, during a stint at Air Command and Staff College, with more than 500 fellow officers in attendance, all in Class-A blue uniforms.

EMERGENCIES

One night, when making a max-gross-weight takeoff, a right-engine fire warning light illuminated. Since we were 10 knots below the chart-predicted refusal speed, and the B-57 can be a handful to fly on one engine, I made an instant decision to abort the takeoff. The end of our runway was coming up fast, and brakes were applied as firmly as I dared to avoid locking up the wheels—but we weren't slowing down. I stomped harder to blow the tires and stop short of the airfield lighting stanchions.

Damn! No matter how hard I hammered the brake pedals, the wheels wouldn't lock up and the tires wouldn't blow. We rolled through the light stanchions—under-wing bombs and full tip tanks somehow missing them all—and finally stopped in the runway overrun. As I stop-cocked the engines, I ordered my GIB (Guy in Back, the sensor systems operator) to prepare for egress. As the canopy started coming up, I glimpsed one-each highly motivated GIB running past my cockpit! How he squeezed through that small gap between the barely open canopy and rail is still a mystery.

Turns out that the fire warning light was illuminated by a short in the fire-warning circuit. Further, we later learned the flight manual refusal speed was optimistic. The charts were based on estimates, not flight test data, thanks to fast-track modifications to the G model.

Another night, Dave and I suffered a complete hydraulic system failure, while flying over Laos. The B-57 can be flown without hydraulics, but there's no hydraulic boost for the rudder, and the landing gear and brakes rely on emergency back-up systems. We headed for home and alerted the ground crew that we would be stopping on the runway, using emergency braking. Bombs were jettisoned, we landed and rolled out, slowing on the left side of the runway, after emergency brake pressure was depleted.

Because the B-57 canopy is very heavy, it either could be jettisoned or opened hydraulically with an exterior hand pump. Replacement canopies were not readily available, so I opted for the hand-pump routine. While the ground crew frantically pumped and pumped, the cockpit was heating up smartly— and the canopy wasn't budging. Did I mention that it was getting really hot? Finally, after about the third manual pumper took over, the canopy unlocked and slooooowly opened. The night air wasn't exactly cool, but far better than our B-57 oven.

I never did learn what caused our hydraulic problem. A postflight maintenance inspection said that we hadn't taken any ground fire. G-model gremlins....

DODGING BULLETS AT NIGHT

Anti-aircraft artillery was always prevalent throughout our operating area. Since the enemy typically used tracer rounds at night, it was relatively easy to maneuver clear of the five- or seven-round bursts. Even though Dave, my GIB, didn't like his sensor-aiming efforts being disrupted, he conceded that my wild gyrations were necessary to keep the jet in one piece.

Of course, to execute those life-saving maneuvers, we first had to spot the bad guys' tracers. The closest I came to being nailed was over several major road intersections near Tchepone, Laos. The first clue that we were being targted was the entire cockpit suddenly glowed bright red. No, we weren't on fire. A stream of seven 57-mm tracers was streaking almost straight up, directly in front of my right wing. That got my attention! And the ensuing violent maneuver to avoid a gunner's subsequent burst got Dave's attention. And it seriously hacked us off. We came back around and did precisely what we'd been cautioned not to do: look for those guns. Dave spotted them with his FLIR, I delivered a message in the form of a funny bomb, and we dutifully departed the area.

Another close call was logged right after we entered our work areas from the west, around 20,000 feet. There were a lot of aircraft inflight every night, and with no air traffic control in that region, see-and-avoid was the rule. Consequently, I normally kept the jet's exterior lights and anti-collision beacons on, until we were below 10,000 feet. One night, as we descended through 8,000 feet, over an area that had always been completely benign, four 57-mm guns—two on each side of our nose—opened up. I instantly rolled inverted, frantically flipping off light switches.

Dave was head-down, eyeballing his system's scope to locate a prominent curve in a river and tweak his sensors. "What the hell are you doing?" he yelled. I was too busy to answer, intent on diving under those flaming rounds. Fortunately, the enemy gunners didn't fire a follow-up salvo.

Yet another valuable lesson was logged between my ears: Do NOT imitate a Christmas tree, when flying into enemy territory!

However, those gunners had a few more lessons awaiting unsuspecting flight crews. Throughout most of my combat tour, our enemy typically fired tracer rounds. Thus, AAA (anti-aircraft artillery) was visible and generally avoidable. That is, until the night a smaller-caliber 23-mm changed tactics. I hated those 23-mm monsters. They consisted of four co-mounted guns, each capable of an eye-watering rate of fire. They could put considerably more lead into the sky with each burst than did larger-caliber guns. Again, I normally could deal with them, because their tracers were visible. That warm-and-fuzzy aspect evaporated, when we were fragged to a traditionally quiet area in southern Laos.

Cruising at about 3,000 feet over pitch-black jungle, with Dave scanning for targets, 23-mm rounds suddenly exploded all around us. No tracers! That got my serious attention, and we hauled out of there immediately.

During post-strike debriefing back at Ubon, I reported being engaged by tracerless 23-mm AAA. Intelligence officers said I must have imagined that, because nobody had ever reported the enemy firing tracerless

23-mm. Two nights later, though, the pre-mission intel briefer cautioned, "You might encounter tracerless 23-mm in that area of Laos." Apparently, I was the first to report it, but not the last. Luckily, I never saw the nasty stuff again.

MY ONLY MISSION WORKING WITH ANOTHER FAC

In the late winter of '71, Dave and I headed for our designated work area in central Laos, a zone that had been devoid of targets. As I checked in with Moonbeam, our ABCCC (Airborne Battlefield Command and Control Center), I heard a Covey FAC (an O-2 from Pleiku Air Base) requesting ordnance on a target he had located in southern Laos. Since few targets were in our assigned work area, I called Moonbeam and volunteered our services. Such an on-the-fly mission-area change rarely was approved by controllers, but they said "go for it" and passed the Covey's coordinates and contact frequency.

The FAC said he'd located a suspected truck park and storage facility near the Mekong River. For weeks, Covey FACs had been monitoring truck traffic going into an area obscured by heavy jungle canopy, but saw none coming out. They suspected the NVA were stockpiling ammunition, POL and supplies there, because the river was too high to easily cross, due to winter storms.

As we approached the designated area, I discussed the situation with the Covey. Locked onto his scope, Dave suddenly yelled that he'd found a batch of trucks on a valley trail, "running like cockroaches, when someone turned on the lights!" We immediately went to work. The Covey FAC orbited over a nearby ridge, calling out AAA sites, as we made multiple attacks on the frantic 'roaches. An LGB dropped on the lead truck bottled up the trail, halting the caravan. A series of funny bombs on the other trucks and the storage area triggered huge explosions and widespread fires. We soon called "Winchester" (all weapons expended) and prepared to depart. However, that Covey kept calling in additional strikes, which continued for another full day. The Covey's subsequent BDA (Bomb Damage Assessment) report of our mission was six trucks destroyed, fifteen major secondary explosions and smaller secondary explosions "too numerous to count."

An interesting small-world element from that mission: After telling Moonbeam we were checking-out and heading for home, a familiar voice came over the air. "Is that you Ad?" A pilot that I'd been stationed with two years prior had recognized my voice. He later came to Ubon for an enjoyable mini-reunion.

A few days after that successful mission, a post-strike BDA photo was posted in our Wing briefing room, stamped "SECRET." It clearly showed truck hulks, burned out fuel drums and all manner of debris from the destroyed storage area. But since it was classified, I couldn't get a copy of the photo. A few weeks later, I was flipping through a magazine that someone had left in our squadron lounge. There was the identical picture, without classification markings, that had been posted in our intel shop. A simple caption stated: "USAF aircraft destroyed a major NVA storage area." Assuming I could keep that one, I ripped it out.

TIME TO LEAVE

As the end of our combat tour approached, commanders were confronted with a dilemma. The B-57G's unique capabilities were still in demand, but, technically, the entire squadron was eligible to rotate back to the States. Everybody had flown in at the same time, so we supposedly could all fly out at the same time. Some had to stay, though. Cambodia was heating up and the B-57Gs ultimately saw action there.

Nevertheless, a plan to stagger our departures was needed. In the early spring of '71, the commander convened a meeting to execute a high-tech process for deciding who went home and when: drawing numbers from a hat. I drew number two, which meant I would be the second guy to leave, despite being on-site only nine months. Still, I had logged more than 100 missions, and replacement crews were starting to show up in the squadron.

Shortly thereafter, I boarded a big, beautiful C-130 and took off from Ubon as a passenger, not a combat pilot. The jet I'd flown to the base months before stayed behind, waiting for another crew to continue the battle. It had served me well.

Ad Thompson graduated in the U.S. Air Force Academy's third class (1961). After pilot training, he was assigned to Air Defense Command, Air Training Command and Tactical Air Command. He flight tested the B-57G Tropic Moon system at MacDill and Eglin AFBs, Florida, before deploying to Ubon RTAB, Thailand, and flying 105 combat missions. Later, he

B-57 Canberras en route to Vietnam

attended Air Command & Staff College, then USAF Test Pilot School. He spent the remainder of his USAF career as a test pilot and flight test project manager on myriad development programs, including two prototype jets. He headed several combined test forces and commanded a remote detachment of Edwards AFB. After retiring from the USAF, he spent 20 years as a civilian test pilot, ultimately serving as chief B-1B test pilot and Director of Flight Test for Rockwell International. Following Rockwell's merger with Boeing, he was named Director of Flight Test for Boeing's X-32 Joint Strike Fighter candidate. (Photos: Ad Thompson)

KILLING TRAINS

Ed Rasimus

(Excerpted from *When Thunder Rolled: An F-105 Pilot over North Vietnam*)

A Republic F-105 Thunderchief loaded with Mark 82 500-pound bombs taxis prior to a combat mission. During the mid-1960s, "Thuds" were the Air Force's primary strike fighter over North Vietnam.

Republic Aviation Corporation

Our target for the day was a bridge at Bac Ninh on the northeast railroad. Ingress could be along the mountainous coast, and the only heavy defenses were along the railroad itself and in the flatlands where the narrow valley that harbored the rail line opened up on the Delta. I was flying wing on Major Bill Loyd, with the new assistant operations officer, Major Ken Frank, flying as number three and Karl Richter as four. Our load was five Mark 83 low-drag bombs. Rain the night before hinted that the monsoon was overhead and the only weather factor was going to be local. The target area several hundred miles north of us would be reasonably clear.

As the gear and flaps of my F-105 Thunderchief were coming up on takeoff, the weak howling of an emergency beeper on Guard channel played as background to the routine radio chatter. We climbed to 18,000 feet and went to a tactical spread formation. Loyd asked Invert (a ground-control intercept or GCI site) if they were getting a beeper, and the depressing reply confirmed it had been a bad morning already. The first strike package, primarily out of Tahkli, but with support from other bases, had five airplanes down. Before Loyd could ask about rescue efforts, Invert advised that all five were down in the flats over the Red River, and only one had a pending rescue effort ongoing.

Single-seat airplanes leave you alone with your thoughts. So, I cruise, bomb-laden and on autopilot, across Laos and the panhandle to the deep blue water of the Gulf of Tonkin, arms draped on canopy rails, looking left and right, watching the scenery and thinking. The beepers come and go in the background, and each time you hear it, you wonder if you should shut off Guard, or if it will go away in a minute or two. You wonder who is down and how it happened. Are they alive or dead? Inevitably, you wonder what others would think if it were your beacon. Would they be cruising comfortably in the morning sun or would they be doing something for you? What could you be doing now? Nothing. You're too far away. You have a target to go to. There's a tanker coming up, you're just a wingman and you have a job to do.

We switch channels and talk to Panama, a GCI site on Monkey Mountain near Danang. They point us at Brown Anchor 31, the lead tanker in a cell of four. Brown 31 is 80 miles north of us and heading our way. We'll pass left-shoulder to left-shoulder, if we continue, but we'll be doing a fighter turn-on rendezvous, meaning that at around 25 mi., we'll start a left turn to trail the tanker.

I call, "Parrot Two's got visual, left 11 o'clock at thirty."

Panama verifies. "Parrot, that's your tanker."

Loyd glances my way momentarily, then back at the spot I've indicated on the horizon. "Parrot's judy," he calls, indicating we'll complete the rendezvous ourselves, without help from Panama. We hold steady for a count of five, then enter a smooth left turn, sliding into refueling position behind the tanker.

Just before I turn my radar to standby, I watch the show of flights appear as blips across my radar scope. We're all going to targets along the northeast railroad, with several flights heading to the Bac Ninh bridge and others hitting various choke points along the line.

We get our gas and drop off the tanker at the north end of the track. The incessant howling of that emergency beeper has stopped, and I don't know whether that means the poor guy has been captured, the battery has gone dead or he's evading and simply turned it off to save power. I hope it's the latter, but deep inside, I suspect the worst. No one gets picked up from Route Pack VI.

As we cruise up the Gulf at 20,000 feet, I sweep the coastline, my radar painting a map of the landfall ahead and the easy-to-find pork chop-shaped island that sits on our nose. We'll turn inbound at the south tip of the island, a prominent point that's easy to find visually—or if the weather had been bad, using our radar. The North Vietnamese know we use the island for navigation, so they'll undoubtedly welcome us with a barrage of 37- and 57-mm. flak. It's always too low and always bursts behind us, but one of these days, they're bound to get lucky.

Rather than head straight for the target, we're going to angle north, working our way along the 20-mi. buffer zone with China's border. That will keep us clear of many SAM sites along the usual route to Kep and the railroad. We'll attack, then turn east and outbound at Bac Ninh. We'll spend most of the ingress at 4,000-6,000 feet above the ground, then pop up to about 12,000 feet for our dive-bomb pass.

We descend and turn left at the coast. My Doppler's set to the coordinates of an intersection of the railroad and buffer zone. Our flight is spread and nearly line abreast, almost a mile wide, and humping over the dark-green jungle at 540 knots. That's 9 miles/minute, an easy number for the mental math needed to judge time-to-go to the target. Once we get close, we'll push up to 600 knots, giving us plenty of energy for the popup. On our way out, we really won't care what our speed is; we just want to get back into formation and watch for SAMs and enemy MiGs.

White puffy clouds and the dark-blue morning sky contrast with the deep emerald green of jungle hills. Gray karst formations rise from the foliage, creating a beautiful landscape below. Our airplanes ride smoothly, and for a moment, sheer exhilaration is enough to blank out the fact that this is war, we are deep in enemy territory and in a moment, all hell is going to break loose. We're going to rain death and destruction down on an enemy who is going to be trying extremely hard to stop us. Two minutes to the turn point.

There it is. The railroad is in sight, in a narrow cut in the mountains barely 3 miles wide. Now the turn down to Bac Ninh. Wait. What's that? We're over the tracks and below us is a rail siding. No, it's two sidings along the main line. A small rail yard, right here at the buffer zone.

And there are two trains filling the tracks. A small station house sits on the east side of the tracks. In an instant, I picture tired engineers who've parked their trains, knowing even better than we pilots overhead that the rules of engagement (ROEs) call this a "buffer zone." They're probably in the station house, talking over a cup of coffee about the night's run into or out of Hanoi with their freight of war materials.

I call, "Parrot Two has a pair of trains on the tracks right below us," not sure what we're going to do about it.

Loyd doesn't hesitate. "Roger, tally-ho. Coming left. We'll roll in to the north and off right, outbound. One'll be up in ten."

Alright! We're going to hit something real! I'm on the inside of the turn and start to slide behind lead as he comes around. I watch his afterburner light and the plane's nose come up. I cut the corner, behind his flight path, throw the throttle outboard and feel the nozzles open, then the push as that burner lights.

The bangs of our afterburners have drawn the attention of those trainmen. Guns around the rail yard start to flash and puffs of 37-mm. begin to appear low and to my left as I hit 12,000 feet, then roll inverted to pull down on the target. The trains are under my pipper and I can see Loyd's bombs going off. They've exploded near the north end of the trains, so I adjust toward the center of a string of boxcars.

A huge plume of white smoke erupts, as one of the engineers apparently throws full throttle to his locomotive, but he's already trying to drag derailed wreckage down broken tracks. I mash on the pickle button and feel the jolts of bombs coming off, then pull and look for lead's aircraft. He's in a hard right turn, coming to one o'clock and climbing. I set my cutoff and look back to see three and four coming off the target.

Loyd keeps his rejoin turn going until he's parallel to the railroad, then reverses to head outbound. We're back into our spread and clear of the flak in less than a minute. Outbound, a strange notion enters my head. This is fun. It's a rush, a thrill, a challenge to do something that most people can't even conceive and couldn't do, even if they wanted to. Parrot flight is roaring across the countryside, headed for the coast and a weird idea enters my head. It suddenly occurs to me that what we're doing is a lot like stealing hubcaps.

When I was growing up in Chicago, guys in the neighborhood would occasionally decide that we needed to steal some hubcaps. We would talk about what style was particularly cool and make a choice—Lincoln spinners or Plymouth cones or maybe even after-market custom jobs like chrome Moons. Then we'd scout the neighborhood streets until we found a likely target. Four guys would approach the car late at night, then, one to a wheel, crouch down to pop off the cap. Invariably, one would be dropped, making a huge noise. That would alert the car owner, usually a big, burly, blue-collar kind of guy in a sleeveless undershirt with a can of beer in his hand. He'd turn on the porch light and scream, "Hey, what youse guys doing dere?" We'd take off running, and maybe he would chase us.

We didn't need the hubcaps. We merely wanted the chase, the adrenaline rush of tweaking some poor working stiff's nose and getting chased. Now, we're a whole lot faster—and what we're doing is in the name of national policy—but each morning we decide what kind of "hubcaps" we're going to steal for the day. Then we plan our strategy and sneak into a Vietnamese neighborhood, sometimes at low altitude, sometimes by a circuitous route. Then we grab the prize and run away. If we get chased a bit, that's so much the better, as long as we don't get caught. We wind up with a huge rush and a release that leaves us chattering and swaggering for hours afterward. Then we sleep and the next morning we do it again. Some are convinced it's patriotism, doing our part for the security of the free world, but henceforth, I'll always recognize it as stealing hubcaps.

At the coast, we head south to a post-strike tanker, then back across the panhandle of North Vietnam to Korat, Thailand. After landing, we're still feeling pumped about the results of our strike and are eager to get to debriefing. Cold air conditioning in the command post does little to quell our enthusiasm—until the tech-sergeant intel debriefer raises an eyebrow during our strike report. He excuses himself and charges down the hall, returning with the chief of intel, Lieutenant Colonel Winter.

"What'd you guys do?" Winter asks.

We recount our ingress plan and our luck at finding the trains. We describe our attack and each of us confirms an estimate that at least three-quarters of our bombs hit the two trains or the tracks. We're fairly certain we didn't get either of the engines, but we estimate at least forty boxcars were destroyed and all of the tracks cut. We point to a map where the attack took place. The white-haired intel officer shakes his head and grimly observes that it looks as though our strike was in the China-buffer zone.

"It looks like you've busted the ROE," he announces.

"What does that mean?" Loyd inquires. "We're authorized to maneuver in the buffer zone, aren't we?"

"Sure," replies Winter, "but you aren't supposed to strike targets in the zone. It's a sanctuary to make sure we don't inadvertently drop anything in China."

"Yeah, but isn't it clear they're using that ROE to protect their trains, and where we struck is definitely in North Vietnam?" Richter wants to know.

"Doesn't matter. You can't drop in the buffer."

Winter suggests we take a look at our flight data again. "What did you use to establish the coordinates you gave us? How did you determine the location of the drop?"

I volunteer that I was using Doppler coordinates for the intersection of the railroad and the buffer zone. It looked to me like we were 2 mi. north of the intersection when we hit those tracks. Ken Frank says he was trying to use Red Crown TACAN, a navigation station on a U.S. destroyer in the Gulf. The signal was intermittent that far inland and he wasn't too sure of the radial and distance. Richter thinks his Doppler might have shown us right at the intersection. Loyd looks at each of us then turns to Winter.

"I think our initial plot might have been a bit off. Let me see that map again. Sure, here we are, right near this peak and just past this little village. That's right, here's where the siding is. It's about two miles south of the buffer zone. Don't you agree?" He polls the members of the flight. We all nod enthusiastically.

The senior intel officer has seen this before. He hints at a smile and says, "I thought so. Nice job, guys." He initials the report and returns to his office.

During the Vietnam War, the late-Ed Rasimus flew more than 250 combat missions in F-105s and F-4s, receiving the Silver Star, Distinguished Flying Cross five times, and numerous Air Medals. He later worked for Northrop on the YF-23 advanced tactical fighter program, wrote several books and taught political science.

THE THREAT INSIDE MY AIRCRAFT
Tom Menza

December 1969

Another day, another mission. From Saigon, my crew and I routinely hauled critical cargo all over South Vietnam. Our lumbering, 1950s-vintage C-123K transport wasn't sexy, but the old girl was a vital link to troops depending on us to bring them beans, bullets, bombs and priceless letters from home. We routinely dodged ground fire, but never in my wildest dreams could I have anticipated today's bizarre mission.

Lieutenant Tom Menza in his C-123K's front office
Tom Menza

During preflight, I noticed the ground crew spreading hay and straw on the cargo bay's floor. *What the...?* A large truck backing up to the aircraft's lowered rear ramp brought the answer: A 2,000-pound Asian water buffalo.

We were tasked with flying the U.S. State Department's four-legged, one-ton gift to a Vietnamese village, where a local militia had helped U.S. Army Rangers protect a mountain pass. A dozen handlers wrestled the beast up the loading ramp, pushing and pulling it to a midship position.

Our reluctant passenger was rigid, tense and breathing heavily, resisting the crew's diligent attempts to wrap a web of six nylon straps around his massive form and tie them to anchor rings in the floor. I hoped the hay and straw would absorb water buffalo droppings and urine. Otherwise, our maintenance guys' corrosion control team would rip me a new one.

Southeast Asian water buffalo

Once the critter was secured, my crew and I boarded via the forward entry door to avoid our guest in the cargo bay. We strapped into the cockpit, completed routine checks and procedures, started engines and taxied to the end of the runway.

"Saigon Tower, Bookie one-zero-five, number-one on taxiway Alpha for departure."

"This is Saigon. Bookie on Alpha, cleared for takeoff." Our flight engineer pushed the throttles up to takeoff power and we rolled. The usual rattling and considerable vibration eventually disappeared, as our steed left the ground. The miracle of flight had happened again.

We climbed to 5,000 feet and settled in for the 40-minute flight to our destination—an 1,800-foot dirt airstrip on top of a hill, adjacent to a small village surrounded by large, tropical trees. None of us would forget that village. Its name was distinctive and, as it turned out, quite appropriate for the day's mission: Phuoc Yu. *"Ph"* is pronounced as an *"F"*.

En route, I enjoyed the view of Vietnam from above—verdant, laced with rivers and canals, farmers' fields, rolling hills, valleys, villages and a small city or two. Hardly the image of a war zone. Ten minutes before landing, though, serenity gave way to absolute chaos in the back. Our massive passenger was bellowing loudly, accompanied by a cacophony of hooves stomping on the cargo bay's metal floor.

Over the intercom: "Loadmaster to pilot! That damn buffalo got loose!" We now had a one-ton, very angry creature running from one end of our airplane to the other. With its newfound freedom, the critter did what a male water buffalo does—assert its alpha bull status, by targeting the nearest source of its discomfort: our loadmaster.

"*Yiiieee!* Load to pilot! The damn thing is charging me!" he screamed. I glanced over my shoulder to see our loadmaster scramble up the cargo bay's side panels, then cling to the ceiling, barely clear of slashing horns. "Load's" relatively safe haven high in the tail section left him hanging upside down on steel-wire control cables, emulating a tree sloth.

Up-front, the copilot, flight engineer and I tried to remain inconspicuous, silently thanking Him that we weren't back there with Big Buff and our load-sloth. Besides, we had our hands full, fighting to maintain control of the airplane.

"Descent check!" I called, setting up to land. Of course, nothing in our kneepad checklists covered landing with a runaway water buffalo bellowing, stomping, ramming bulkheads and trying to destroy the insides of an aircraft. Its awesome horns had already punctured the aircraft skin. We had to get on the ground ASAP!

Landing on a short field required full flaps and the slowest-possible safe airspeed, a couple of knots above stall. That was about 89 knots, as I recall.

Using the FM radio, my copilot called a Special Forces team holding the airstrip. "Phuoc Yu radio, Bookie one-zero-five. Random overhead to three-zero, full stop."

I turned final and lined up with the runway, aiming for a near-end touch down point a thousand feet below. At such a slow landing speed, trimming the aircraft was crucial. That meant balancing aerodynamic forces on the flight controls with a large "trim wheel" linked by cables to tabs on the aft edge of our horizontal tail. Trimming reduced the amount of control force a pilot felt. By not having to manhandle the C-123K's heavy, unboosted controls, trimmed landings were easier and safer.

However, at a mere 500 feet, just before landing, that loud, bellowing buffalo decided to lumber from the back to the front of the cargo bay. That one-ton shift of weight drastically altered the aircraft's center-of-gravity, unbalancing my landing trim setting. As the bull ran fore and aft, the aircraft nose went up and down, requiring constant power and speed changes to compensate for pitch variations. We were now in a no-win cycle. Adding speed to avoid stalling and regain pitch control meant we were too fast to stop on the short Phuoc Yu dirt strip. Unable to land, I rammed the throttles forward, pulled the nose up and executed a go-around. Circling back, I tried again. The damned critter moved again, and my trim and pitch control went wild. Again! Add power and make another go-around.

Five landing attempts. Five go-arounds.
Barry Griffiths /flickr.com

We attempted five landings, and made five go-arounds. There was no way we were going to land with a water buffalo racing around back there, punching holes in our aircraft's aluminum skin. Sooner or later, the blasted critter's horns were going to destroy something critical and we'd crash. Splatting in front of Phuoc Yu's elders and our State Department host would be embarrassing.

A strange thought flashed through my brain, as we circled the field for yet another landing attempt. A year ago, I'd been flying a sleek supersonic jet, strapped into a snug, compact cockpit. Now I'm trying to control a flying barn with a wild water buffalo on the loose!

Think! Maybe I could drop our out-of-control passenger. Lower the tail ramp, open the rear ramp door, yank the aircraft's nose up and let that damned buffalo *sliiiiide* out. But a quick glance to the rear scrubbed that idea. What if those hungous horns got stuck in the rigging or door frame? Then we'd have the beast dangling outdoors, acting as a giant air brake. *No dice*, I thought. Having no performance data for asymmetric water buffalo swinging from one side of the fuselage, I ruled out dumping the beast.

I glanced at the crew's aluminum gun box. There were four M-16 military rifles in there. The flight engineer looked at me and grinned. An experienced hunter from Montana, he asked and I granted permission to "take him out. Aim to the back or the side of the airplane, not up here and not toward the ceiling," I warned. The loadmaster was still up there, playing sloth. Briefing complete.

"Copy!" the clearly motivated engineer said. He climbed down to the cargo bay, opened the gun box, grabbed an M-16, and went hunting. *Bam! Bam!* Two shots, followed by considerable bellowing, hoof-stomping, and a flight engineer cursing and shouting over the intercom.

"Geez, I winged it! *Aw shit!* He's charging!"

The copilot shouted, "Shoot at the head! Head shot! Now! Now, dammit!"

Bam! A loud, heavy thud. Silence. Big Boy Beast was down, less than a yard from the flight engineer, who was sporting an ear-to-ear grin. Our courageous, big-game-hunter crewmate had just shot an attacking water buffalo inside our airplane, using a military-grade semi-automatic rifle. This was undoubtedly a first in hunting lore, and a potential cover story for both *"Guns and Ammo"* and *"Aviation Week & Space Technology."* Definitely a two-fer!

I landed safely, taxied to a dirt parking area just off the runway, and ran through the engine shutdown checklist. The loadmaster unwound from his safe perch among the rigging, performed his after-landing duties, and lowered the tail ramp, constantly mumbling about being in a "damned combat zone, taking hits from a damned water buffalo, inside a damned airborne airplane." PTSD wasn't a term we used back then, but our loadmaster had it.

Villagers and ground troops crowded around the back, gawking wide-eyed at the mess inside. They knew something unusual had been going on, when we aborted several landing attempts.

Apologetically, I explained to the gathering that we couldn't land with Big Boy running around inside. We would have crashed. So, we had to kill the poor thing. It was the only humane option…for our well-being. The villagers nodded gravely, though no one understood English. Too bad, so sad. But tonight they'd enjoy buffalo steak.

They pulled the beast out with ropes, and kindly swept up the hay, straw and buffalo manure. We bade the villagers, Army troops and a stunned State Department guy so-long and boarded our somewhat beat up bird. The flight back to base was uneventful and quiet, as each crew member tried to assimilate what we'd just experienced. I landed, taxied to our parking ramp, and shut everything down.

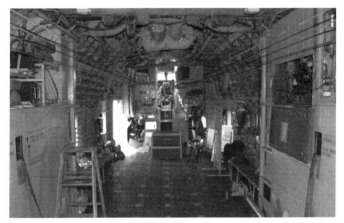

C-123K cargo bay, looking forward
U.S. Air Force

I dutifully filled out flight and maintenance logs, noting "small-arms holes in aircraft skin, starboard side of cabin." Taking small-arms hits was a weekly routine for our operations, improving the odds that maintenance would never question new holes.

I was dragging tail. Time to call it a day and head for the crew quarters. I looked forward to a shower, clean clothes, a good dinner in the chow hall, and hitting the rack. Soon, details of the day's surreal flight—graced with images of a crazed water buffalo puncturing holes in my airplane—faded away. I quickly fell asleep around 10 p.m.

About midnight, I was awakened by loud knocking at the door. Our maintenance officer, carrying an aircraft log book, wandered in, wearing a sheepish grin. "Ah, lieutenant, you wrote in this log, 'Possible ground fire…'"

"That's right, sir," I quickly confirmed.

"Well, lieutenant…. Yes, there were bullet holes in the cabin skin." He hesitated, still grinning. "But with the metal bending outward, not inward. Those holes were made by rounds fired from inside your airplane."

Busted. I spent the rest of the night filling out paper work and debriefing maintenance and intelligence folks about the art of shooting an uncontrolled water buffalo inside an almost-uncontrollable C-123K.

Tom Menza's C-123K proudly announced the birth of its pilot's first son.

After completing U.S. Air Force pilot training in 1969, Tom Menza was assigned to the 19th Special Operations Squadron in Saigon, South Vietnam, flying the C-123K, an ugly troop transport. His 22 years on active duty included flying KC-135 tankers, serving in staff assignments and teaching at the Air Force Academy. After retiring from military service, he attended law school and practiced law in Colorado for 30 years. Occasionally, he returned to the cockpit as a part-time charter and business jet pilot. Retiring from everything in 2017, he now enjoys well-earned time with his wife at home… and sleeping-in late.

U.S. MARINE 'SCOOTER'
"HAWK"

The typhoon hit Kadena Air Force Base, Okinawa, around 2000, while my fellow travelers and I were eating supper at the officers' club. By the time we finished, the wind was howling, topping 100 knots. Our rooms in the Bachelors Officers Quarters (BOQ) were about 500 yards away. Surely we could make it that far. Wrong. We couldn't begin to make headway against that gale, so we hunkered down and spent the next two days in the club, sleeping on the floor, playing ace-deuce and contemplating our future.

Welcome to the war, I thought, staring at impenetrable sheets of rain, driven by winds unlike any I'd encountered in the States. Hard to believe I'd departed those States only a few days ago. With nothing else to do, I mentally retraced the long road from college student to my role today, a U.S. Marine Corps fighter pilot on the cusp of putting hard-won training to the ultimate test: Air combat.

Systematic training and development of combat-ready skills were accomplished through multiple deployments to stateside weapons-training bases. Although everybody in our unit was headed for Vietnam, I didn't go overseas with my classmates. I was tapped for an additional few months of Military Operation Specialities (MOS) training—formal schools that added nuclear weapons and forward air control expertise to my A-4 Skyhawk fighter pilot "resume."

That graduate training was crammed into my last few months in the U.S., eating into precious time spent with family—and relocating them—prior to being deployed. Thanks to a shortage of military housing, families were not allowed to remain in base quarters, while active-duty guys went overseas. My bride and I decided she'd move back to our hometown, close to family support.

After securing those extra MOS credentials, getting my family settled, and saying goodbye to everybody, I hopped a flight to San Francisco, orders and transportation tickets in-hand. I only carried a sea bag full of uniforms and a few creature comforts. The next challenge was getting from San Francisco International to Travis Air Force Base, about 60 miles northeast. After several en route glitches, such as arcane bus transfers, I checked in at the Travis Air Force Base (AFB) transit lounge. My assigned charter flight to Kadena AFB, Okinawa, wasn't leaving until the next day. So, I hit the sack—on the lounge floor.

The next morning, a gaggle of us boarded a Continental Boeing 707—"Proud Bird with the Golden Tail"—for a long flight around the Pacific Rim. A refueling stop in Alaska was brief, because the Continental aircrew was racing a typhoon aimed at Okinawa. That afternoon, we landed at Kadena, where buses ferried us to Camp Hansen. We checked in at the BOQ and did a touch-and-go at Administration to have orders stamped and be scheduled for flights on to Da Nang, Republic of Vietnam (RVN). Off to the Officers Club for evening chow…and there we sat for three days, watching that typhoon batter Okinawa.

The gale-force winds finally died down to around 50 knots, enabling a dash for the BOQ and much-needed showers. Three days behind schedule, we boarded a C-130 Hercules headed for Da Nang. Post-landing, the C-130 crew lowered the aft ramp, while taxiing to the transit line. An unbelievable blast of hot air, stifling humidity and the aroma of burning crappers smacked us in the face. We checked in with admin, had our orders endorsed, and were given a C-ration at the transit facility.

An admin guy pointed to several hundred folding cots spread across a hanger floor. "Make yourself at home. Any open cot," he said. We also were shown the camp's out-houses, piss tubes, and protective trenches to dive into, during mortar attacks. Intense heat, swarms of mosquitoes and an early morning mortar barrage ensured nobody slept that night.

Around noon the next day—again soaked with perspiration—we boarded a Douglas C-47 for a flight to Chu Lai, a Marine air base about forty miles south of Da Nang. Fifty-some years after leaving that stifling Vietnam heat, I still have memories of rare little comforts. Like the cool, refreshing air, shortly after our C-47 took off and climbed to altitude.

We landed on Chu Lai's 4,000-foot airstrip, made of steel Marsden matting, and debarked into even more-oppressive heat and humidity. I was met by John, a good friend with whom I'd gone through flight school. We'd also been together through our first duty assignment. He had departed the states two months before I did, thanks to the additional MOS schools I'd attended. Per custom, John was my designated "sponsor," a Marine charged with making sure I checked all the required new-guy boxes: orders endorsed, forms filled out, supplies issued, assigned to a squadron, intel and operations briefings given, and an orientation tour of the base completed.

Chu Lai Marine Base in 1966. Built of Marsden matting, only 4,000 feet were initially operational.
"Hawk"

John wrapped up by escorting me to the billeting area, where I was assigned a cot in a hard-back tent shared with five other Marines. My new home. Supper at the mess tent consisted of "B" rations, which really weren't too bad, thanks to the Marine cooks' ingenuity. Sorry, no ice.

After supper, John excused himself, noting that he was on the night's flight schedule. That was the last time I ever saw him. John was shot down on that mission, 40 miles West of Chu Lai.

Welcome to RVN reality.

A short runway dictated making jet-assisted takeoffs, when fully loaded.
U.S. Marine Corps

The next day, I was armed with a trusty A-4 Skyhawk, ready to save the world from communism. Nicknamed the "Scooter" or "Heinemann's Hotrod," it was compact and deadly, capable of delivering a full-spectrum of destruction—2,000-, 1,000-, 500- and 250-pound bombs; five-inch Zuni and 2.75-inch rockets with high-explosive warheads; 20-mm cannons, and napalm canisters. The Skyhawk was a versatile combat platform, thanks to stellar performance characteristics. It delivered ordnance accurately, and had the agility to maneuver aggressively in the face of hostile fire.

Our primary mission was close air support (CAS), working with Marine infantry units. When called upon, we rained death and destruction on any hostile force threatening our fellow Marines.

In addition, we were fragged by 7th Air Force to provide "excess" sorties for operational and strategic air missions in our assigned region. These included sorties north of the Demilitarized Zone (DMZ) and in neighboring countries, as required.

The first challenge for new-guy A-4 pilots was mastering the art of launching from Chu Lai's too-short 4,000-foot airstrip. When fully loaded with ordnance, getting a Scooter airborne required an extra kick from a Jet Assisted Takeoff system. Two JATO bottles were attached, one on each side of the aircraft's fuselage, just aft of the wing root. When torched off, these rockets produced 7,000 pounds of thrust for about four seconds, smartly accelerating a jet to liftoff speed. We immediately headed for the South China Sea, where the empty JATO bottles were jettisoned to reduce drag.

Recovering back at Chu Lai dictated making an arrested landing on that short airstrip, following the guidance of a Landing Signal Officer (LSO), as if coming aboard an aircraft carrier. Thanks to Seabee and Marine engineers' diligent efforts to improve its condition, the runway was eventually extended to 8,000 feet.

A freshly minted fighter pilot, I was always ready and excited to fly each and every assigned combat mission. I'd even hang around the ready room at night, hoping to snivel extra sorties, if a pilot canceled for maintenance or other reasons. The most satisfying missions were responding to ground troops in close contact with enemy forces, and being able to turn the tide of battle. Weather conditions often complicated the challenge of putting bombs-on-target close to our guys, but if Marines were in danger of being overrun, we readily "stretched" minimums to help those gutsy grunts.

Fast forward to 9 October 1966. Our squadron had been fragged by

7th Air Force for a number of missions directed by Air Force Forward Air Controllers (Airborne) using call signs "Covey" and "Nail." These were flown in neighboring countries, typically to interdict traffic on the Ho Chi Minh Trail. Once we were on-station, USAF FACs would fire a white phosphorus rocket to mark a target and clear us to drop bombs on or near it. Those targets, more often than not, were in mountainous, heavily forested areas and rarely yielded secondary explosions that would confirm we'd hit something significant. We expended tons of high explosives that did little more than turn big trees into toothpicks.

Douglas A-4 Skyhawk
Curtis Foster

Convinced we were wasting perfectly good high explosives, we started calling "Winchester" (meaning our ordnance had been expended), after dropping a couple of bombs. With weapons still tucked under our wings, we'd start "doing road reconnaissance," attacking targets of opportunity that might have a real impact on the war effort.

Thanks to skill, luck or Providence, my jet had never taken a significant hit from enemy gunners. That stretch ended on a day we flew up the North Vietnam coast and spotted a sizable river (the Gianh) with beaucoup boat traffic near the costal town of Ba Don. Flying northwest, upriver and into mountains near the village of Kim Lich, we hit the jackpot—a string of ten barges tied up along the shore. Our Scooters went to work, successively attacking those barges, until nine of the floating fuel tanks were on fire.

With 20 mm ammo left, we dropped to very low altitude and "road recce'd" back to the coast. One pilot spotted a construction project surrounded by trenches packed with North Vietnamese Army soldiers. As we rolled in, they opened up with 12.7-mm heavy guns and AK-47 small arms. Enough of that! Fight's on!

We circled back, nosed over and promptly dispatched the troops with our 20-mm cannon. I could easily see tracers flying past my aircraft, but I'd also become adept at spotting bullets glinting in the sun, while jinking (maneuvering) smartly to avoid them. Aggressive jinking was directly related to staying alive, and lead slugs homing on one's canopy tended to be incredibly motivating.

After a second attack run, I pulled off-target, glanced inside and noticed the jet's utility and flight control hydraulic system warning lights were illuminated. My wingman joined up and verified that there were holes in my aircraft, fuel was streaming from the wing, and vapor was flowing from the aft fuselage. Without delay, I headed for the coast.

We contacted "Joyride," the air battle coordinator, and requested a tanker. We were vectored toward a C-130 air refueling tanker that generally orbited on-station, during air operations. I hoped to link up, before my fuel tanks went dry.

Silently, I thanked Ed Heinemann, a legendary Douglas Aircraft engineer credited with designing the Skyhawk, for creating a tough, reliable aircraft that could take hits and keep on flying. Without hydraulic fluid, my fighter's flight controls reverted from hydraulic assist to manual mode—cables connected directly to the aircraft's aerodynamic surfaces. To control the bird in pitch and roll, I had to muscle a very stiff control stick, but it was manageable. At least when flying straight and level.

Aerial refueling was a different matter. Hitting a trailing-hose basket with the A-4's refueling probe could be a challenge, but manhandling a jet with heavy, sluggish controls was exhausting. I had no choice, though. Either hit that oversized badminton birdie, or run out of fuel, eject and walk home—without being snatched by angry bad guys we'd just hammered. Number One Rule of fighter-flying: Never punch out over troops you'd just bombed and strafed.

After taking on fuel, my wingman and I headed for Chu Lai. Without hydraulic pressure, I couldn't lower the flaps, which meant making a considerably faster-than-normal, no-flap approach and landing. Thankfully, gravity would drop the landing gear, when I pulled a mechanical door release handle. The tail hook also was a gravity-assist design.

C-130 Hercules refueling an A-4 Skyhawk
Rich Benner

I again thanked Ed Heinemann for his foresight.

Luckily, Chu Lai weather gods were smiling and the field was VFR—excellent visibility. The approach and arrested landing were uneventful. I was grateful to be on the ground safe and sound, and elated that the mission was a solid success.

Arrested landings on the short Chu Lai airfield were controlled by a Landing Signal Officer.
U.S. Marine Corps

Non-flyers may not understand, but I was so pumped I couldn't wait to get back in the air. I think all Marine pilots had that attitude. Nothing was more satisfying than being part of a well-trained and motivated group of professional Marine aviators.

During the post-mission debriefing, each pilot somehow forgot to report destroying at least nine fuel barges and sending a batch of enemy troops to Communist paradise. Such oversights occurred with some regularity.

Semper fi!

After completing half of his RVN tour in the A-4, Hawk was reassigned as a Forward Air Controller, then an Air Liaison Officer, attached to a Marine Battalion operating in Northern I Corps, near the Demilitarized Zone. He directed airstrikes by Marine, Navy, Air Force and Army assets per Marine Air Control Doctrine. During a decades-long career, he logged 18,000 hours of flight time in the A-4, F-8 Crusader and numerous multiengine jets. More than 4,000 hours were in the A-4 Skyhawk.

LOCKED ON: TIGER FAC NEARLY NAILS A CELEBRITY*

Skip Holm & William B. Scott

A standard Tiger FAC (Forward Air Control) combat sortie in northern Laos, near the China-North Vietnam border, was buried in secrecy for decades. But why? Fifty years after the mission, records released via the Freedom of Information Act (FOIA) suggested that the FAC crew may have come within seconds of shooting down an American celebrity and notorious anti-war activist. Had they fired, the Vietnam War may have ended much earlier, and hundreds of then-prisoners of war may have survived and come home much sooner.

Vietnam War-vintage F-4E Phantom
Erik Simonsen

The air crew that fateful day, pilot Captain Skip Holm and weapon systems officer Captain RK Brown, were flying a fully armed F-4E Phantom fighter. Deep in enemy territory, the twin-engine fighter was covering 12 miles a minute—four football fields per second—searching for targets and dodging threats. Dense air defense systems' radar continually scanned the sky, probing for American aircraft. To avoid detection by bad-guy radar beams, Holm slipped into a deep canyon and accelerated to high subsonic speeds, his F-4E mere feet above the Mekong River.

Four hours into the mission, Holm and Brown were feeling the strain of constantly dodging threats and threading the chasm's menacing rock walls, looking for supplies coming down the river from China. Tired, low on fuel and 500 miles from Korat Royal Thai Air Base in Thailand, they decided to knock off and head for home. Skip lifted the jet's nose and climbed out of the river canyon, ready to relax a bit.

However, with an unobstructed field of view, Brown's radar immediately detected a target about 50 miles dead ahead, moving southeast, toward Hanoi. It was large, probably an enemy transport of some kind. They immediately called 7th Air Force, reporting the aircraft's location and heading, and requesting permission to shoot the puppy down.

At the time, Tiger FACs operated under strict rules of engagement. Unless fired upon, fighter pilots in the heat of high-speed aerial combat were prevented from shooting at any enemy aircraft, until higher-command approval was received. On-scene air crews had no authority to unilaterally decide which North Vietnamese aircraft were fair game, then attack.

That time-consuming approval process often meant American airmen either were exposed to threats unnecessarily, or missed fleeting opportunities to down enemy aircraft. The only good news: approval could be granted by a single source—7th Air Force War Operations in Saigon. Once approved, the crew rolled in hot and the fight was on. But if approval to fire were denied, a fighter pilot's only option was calling on his Top Gun skills to disengage from the combat arena, without being shot down.

Approvals from 7th Air Force were relayed by a sophisticated Airborne Command and Control Center (ABCCC) aircraft, a Lockheed C-130 that operated as an inflight command post, assessing real-time battlefield situations and routing air support to destroy targets located by FACs.

Nevertheless, the approval process was extremely time-consuming and problematic, when waiting to engage enemy aircraft that didn't hang around long. Like that lone transport Holm's Phantom was locked onto.

In short order, a furious electronic war erupted. North Vietnamese radar operators spotted the American jet closing on the still-unidentified transport aircraft at warp speed. Brown's radar warning scope lit up, alerting him that their Phantom was being illuminated and tracked by enemy radar sites. The bad guys were preparing to blast them from the sky. How and when were the only unknowns.

Time compressed and tension spiked. Analogous to a race horse and jockey poised in the starting gate, Skip and RK chomped at the proverbial bit, waiting with evaporating patience for 7th Air Force's clear-to-fire approval.

Holm jettisoned external fuel tanks and unexpended ordnance, jammed the F-4E's throttles into afterburner, and accelerated to supersonic speed. Onboard combat systems awoke, as RK held the bogey in a TWS (track-while-scan) electronic grip. Skip selectively armed AIM-7 missiles, prepped them for immediate launch and flipped the Master Arm switch.

Come on! Time's running out! They kept pleading with ABCCC operators, reporting that they were in a supersonic tail chase, closing on the slower enemy aircraft at 700 knots. The Phantom would be in missile range very soon, its crew ready to fire and itching to splash that enemy target.

Standby! was 7th's repeated order. Frantic 7th Air Force officials were working hard, trying to determine where the transport had "originated." If it had come from China, shooting down a Chinese aircraft could start a new war. Comparing radar tracks and pop-up targets with a Navy Control unit in the South China Sea was required to verify where the aircraft had taken off.

Skip and RK, warping along at an epic closure rate, were convinced their target had taken off from a North Vietnamese fighter base northwest of Hanoi. It now appeared to be racing toward the city, where it could be protected by the North's fighters. The fact that the enemy's defense posture had come alive with astounding speed seemed to indicate the transport was considered high-value, possibly carrying dignitaries or critical cargo.

What the hell? Where was permission to open fire? A pilot's trigger finger can only hold off for so long!

As if on cue, RK began picking up unmistakable radar signatures that confirmed MiG fighter aircraft were launching from several bases to the F-4's forward and left quadrants. These North Vietnamese fighters were hot to engage the F-4, obviously determined to protect the transport. Skip and RK had to make a decision ASAP: Jump into battle, or break off and run. Skip advised 7th that they had to engage the transport now or RTB (Return To Base). They didn't have enough fuel to fight off a flock of enemy MiGs. Still unable to verify origin of the enemy transport, 7th Air Force issued a "negative" order. Do not fire.

Damn, damn and more damn!

Frustrated, Holm and Brown broke radar lock, banked to the south and headed for Korat. Skip zoomed the Phantom to 40,000 feet and, true to his steed's namesake, vanished from the inbound MiGs' radar scopes.

Some time later, newscasts around the world revealed that Jane Fonda, famous actress and outspoken anti-war activist, had popped up in North Vietnam, pandering to America's enemies and badmouthing the nation that had nurtured her to stardom. Photos surfaced of Fonda donning a North Vietnamese soldier's helmet and sitting on a mobile anti-aircraft gun that allegedly had shot down American fighters.

A group of American prisoners of war were trotted out for Fonda's "inspection" and propaganda photos. Whether naive or outright lying, the actress later claimed the POWs were well-fed and in good condition. A fighter pilot legend claims Fonda shook hands with each POW, and several palmed small slips of paper with notes the men hoped would be passed on to American authorities and loved ones. Fonda reportedly turned each tiny slip of paper over to the North Vietnamese, then departed. Several POWs were subsequently beaten severely, according to former prisoners.

News reports claim that Fonda made two trips to Hanoi, supposedly in July 1972. But she may have been there earlier. Holm and Brown have reason to wonder whether the enemy transport they had locked up, ready to shoot down with AIM-7 Sparrow missiles, was ferrying Jane Fonda to Hanoi.

Had that F-4E combat crew been given clearance to fire, "Hanoi Jane" might never have gained a notoriety that still triggers visceral disgust among Vietnam War veterans and American patriots of any age. How many POWs suffered unspeakable torture, thanks to Jane Fonda's consorting with the enemy, blatantly committing treason? Would the war have ended sooner—or differently—had Fonda not made it to Hanoi? How would history and thousands of lives have been changed, if Skip Holm had fired a couple of missiles, destroying an enemy aircraft possibly carrying a snooty, horribly misguided Hollywood celebrity?

Jane Fonda on a North Vietnamese anti-aircraft gun
Getty Images

KARMIC INTERSECTIONS?

In January 2009, Skip Holm was in Russia, flying and coordinating flight scenes for "Kerosene Cowboys," a modern redux of the hit motion picture, Top Gun. The basic theme was Russia and U.S. forces teamed up to take on terrorists threatening both countries. An undercover squadron comprising Russian and U.S. fighter pilots was formed to fly F/A-18 Hornet, MiG-29 Fulcrum and SU-27 Flanker fighters and take out ISIS terrorists.

Hired to fly those MiG-29s and SU-27s, Skip soon met Troy Garity, a 25-year-old actor on-track to become the new-generation Maverick, Tom Cruise's character in Top Gun. Garity was Jane Fonda's son. The irony of Jane Fonda's kid portraying an heroic American fighter pilot wasn't lost on Skip and his wife, Dede. One evening, the two sat young Garity down and told him exactly why real fighter pilots considered his mother to be a traitor. How Jane had mounted that anti-aircraft gun for propaganda photos. How she had betrayed American POWs, consigning many of them to horrendous torture.

Then, the young actor was stunned to learn how close Skip Holm and

RK Brown had come to blasting his mother out of the sky. "My finger was on the trigger, and it didn't waiver, didn't flinch. If Seventh Air Force had cleared me, I wouldn't have hesitated to take the shot," Skip said. "If your mom had been on that aircraft, she would never have made it to Hanoi. And you wouldn't be here now."

"According to fighter pilot creed, your mom's the only person in the world who can never be truly forgiven," Holm added. "Throughout the Vietnam war, and for years thereafter, the plastic strainer in every urinal on every fighter base had your mom's picture printed on it. Every best-on-earth fighter pilot unzipping an American flight suit enjoyed a li'l sliver of getting-even satisfaction, as he took aim and pissed in Jane Fonda's face. Your mommy's face!"

Skip Holm is credited with logging the most combat flying time of any fighter pilot—1,071 hours—in both the F-105 Thunderchief and F-4 Phantom. He earned 42 combat medals and awards, including three Distinguished Flying Crosses, 25 Air Medals and seven Vietnam Medals. After the war, he was selected for USAF Test Pilot School, then flight tested a variety of aircraft for the Air Force and Lockheed Aircraft. His final Air Force active

duty assignment was in the Philippines, defining the structure for what is now known as Top Gun. As a Lockheed test pilot, Holm flew F-117 Nighthawk development flights, helping bring America's first "stealth fighter" into the USAF inventory. He's also flown myriad aircraft types as a stunt pilot and aerial coordinator for more than 30 movies. A legend in air racing circles, Skip Holm won Unlimited Class gold the first time he competed in the Reno Air Races, and set a still-unbroken race speed record of 512 miles per hour. For that, he was awarded the coveted Thompson Trophy. He now serves as president of Bear Aircraft, which manufactures high-performance, fully acrobatic sport aircraft at a factory in Russia.

* Based on a debriefing account by RK Brown.

SCRAMBLE THE SEAWOLVES!
Sam Feola

7 January 1970

Night. Pitch black, moonless night. Why does bad shit always happen at night?

This particular night shaped the rest of my life. I met Satan that dark night, when we flew directly into a fire-and-brimstone Hell. But he didn't win. With God's help, I survived and walked away a changed man, a man able to handle anything life throws at me. Anything.

I'd been in South Vietnam for two and a half months, assigned to Detachment Seven of Helicopter Attack (Light) Squadron Three (HAL-3), the "Seawolves." Initially, our Det was based at Tay Ninh, a large U.S. Army base in III Corp, adjacent to the Cambodian border. Tay Ninh hosted 3,000 Army soldiers; two Air Force forward air control pilots flying a single-engine Cessna O-1 tail-dragger; and two UH-1B "Huey" gunships crewed by 16 Navy sailors—eight officers (aviators) and eight enlisted door gunners/maintenance gurus. The officers included a Detachment Commander or officer-in-charge, a deputy OIC and six Lieutenant Junior Grade officers. I joined the Seawolves as a 25 year-old Huey pilot fresh from flight school.

The Ho Chi Minh Trail terminated in Cambodia, directly across the river from our base. Day and night, a steady stream of vehicles flowed down that trail, feeding North Vietnamese Army (NVA) Regulars and Viet Cong (VC) troops, weapons, ammunition, food and supplies into South Vietnam. At night, NVA and VC combatants also would sneak across the border in sampans via canals and rivers, then vanish on foot into the jungle.

The Navy's in-country mission was to patrol South Vietnam's waterways and canals, searching for enemy troops and disrupting war materiel transportation and distribution. To that end, the Navy equipped Mobile Riverine Forces' Task Force 116 with armed riverboats. During the day, the boats would stop and search sampans for contraband. At night, the Riverines would lay ambushes at key crossing points. The enemy also set traps for Navy patrol boats in the same areas.

At the beginning of the war, the U.S. Army flew support for Riverine boats that got into firefights or needed other assistance. The Army wasn't always available, because their nearest helicopter units were in Cu Chi,

40 miles away. Army aircrews also weren't instrument-certified, and rarely flew at night or in bad weather.

Consequently, the Navy established a squadron of Huey gunships dedicated to supporting Riverine forces. Nine detachments from the unit were spread throughout III Corps and IV Corps, providing gunship assistance to any American unit that called. In general, we responded to Army units engaged in firefights more often than to Navy patrol boats.

Each squadron detachment was assigned two UH-1Bs that flew together as fire teams. The lead aircraft, piloted by a qualified Attack Helicopter Aircraft Commander (AHAC) in the right seat, served as Fire Team Leader (FTL). His left-seat copilot—in training to become an AHAC—was responsible for the fire team's communications and navigation.

The second helicopter, designated the "trail" ship, was flown by another AHAC who eventually upgraded to be a fire team "lead." His copilot was typically a new aviator who lacked in-country experience. An AHAC could fire seven 2.75-inch rockets from each of two rocket pods, one on each side of the helicopter. The copilot controlled two mini-guns, one on each side, mounted on stub pylons above the rocket pod. Each door gunner manned a free-hand M-60 machine gun fired from the shoulder. Door gunners were tethered by belts to the cabin floor, allowing them to lean out and fire directly ahead, to the side, downward and behind the helicopter. Being a door gunner was an art, and pilots considered them to be the most important elements of a fire team.

Tactically, we flew in offset tandem, about 30 to 50 yards apart. Generally, we flew at an altitude of 1,200 feet to stay out of small arms range and attacked in a dual-ship "daisy chain" or racetrack pattern. During a firefight, the lead ship would descend to 800 feet above ground level (AGL), roll in on the target, start firing at 600 feet and roll off-target to the left at 400-200 feet. The trail ship began its inbound run and started firing rockets, miniguns, and door guns about the time lead rolled off-target. This covered the now-vulnerable lead helo's backside as lead reversed course. Just as the trail ship rolled off-target, lead would begin a second attack run. This enabled putting forward-firing ordnance on-target almost continuously.

Detachment modus operandi was to always be in a ready-to-fly status. Four pilots and four door gunners lived in a Ready Room hooch adjacent to the base's flight line revetments. An Army crank handphone was our link to a nearby command post. We slept in our flight suits and kept zippered—not laced—flight boots close at hand. When called to action, we could be airborne in three minutes.

In December 1969, our Det began flying support missions for Detachment B-41, a Special Forces Green Beret camp at Moc Hoa, located on the west side of the Parrot's Beak, a protrusion of Cambodia into South Vietnam. Moc Hoa sat astride a major VC and NVA infiltration route from Cambodia into South Vietnam. B-41 was one of the most important U.S. Special Forces Camps in Vietnam. Its mission was to disrupt the flow of personnel and VC equipment by interdicting, capturing, or killing the enemy. The camp also housed a detachment of Navy boats that patrolled a web of canals and waterways and helped the Special Forces set ambushes at night.

At the end of December, our detachment was ordered to Ben Luc, a combined South Vietnamese and U.S. Navy base on the Vam Co Dong, a river about 15 miles from Saigon. We moved on Christmas Day and finished unpacking on New Year's Day 1970. We still supported Detachment B-41 at Moc Hoa, but flew from our new base at Ben Luc, about 50 miles away. We were to operate almost exclusively at night, when the enemy was most active.

On one side of the river, an unsecured airfield made of mostly Perforated Steel Plates (PSP) served Army Caribou aircraft flying in personnel, ammunition and supplies. The field had no secured perimeter, allowing anyone—including the VC—to come and go. Besides Army Special Forces and Navy boat crews, Vietnamese Montagnard mercenary operatives lived in a nearby compound. These fearless and ferocious warriors operated on both sides of the Cambodian border. They routinely led Special Forces soldiers into the jungle and guided Navy PBR boats on the river and canals, searching for VC/NVA troops to kill or capture.

To stay clear of fixed-wing Army Caribou takeoffs and landings, our helicopters were kept well off to one side of the PSP runway. We had to operate in the dirt, somewhat equidistant between a bunch of JP-4 fuel bladders and Conex boxes that stored our 2.75-inch rockets and 7.62-mm minigun and M-60 ammunition. Hopefully, we were far enough from both that, during an attack, either the fuel dump or the ammo dump could blow up without taking us out.

A pilot and a door gunner normally would set up a small perimeter between our two helicopters, each manning an M-60 machine gun and M-79 grenade launcher. On this particuar night, all four of us pilots initial-

Armed Seawolf UH-1B "Huey" on alert at Moc Hoa, South Vietnam
Sam Feola

ly hitched a boat ride across the river to the Special Forces outpost for an intelligence briefing. We were told an Army M113 fully tracked armored personnel carrier (APC) mounting a minigun on its center had been captured by the VC a few days earlier. Not good news. However, the operations commander said it had been pretty quiet the last few days, and he wasn't expecting any action that night.

WRONG!

Back at the airfield, most of our team headed up to the compound. Bowles, a door gunner, and I stayed behind, taking our turn at guarding the helos. We opened and ate C-rations for dinner. They weren't bad, as I recall. I especially appreciated the fruit cocktail, fruitcake, Charms candy, and four cigarettes. I became very proficient with a P-38 can opener, and have one to this day.

The unsecured airfield was soon blanketed in pitch-black darkness, guaranteeing we stayed vigilant.

Damn it's dark! Hey! What was that noise...?

Late in the night, as Bowles and I grumbled about such a boring "flight operation," the Fourth of July seemed to explode up-river. The sky was filled with gunfire and rockets. Tracers flying everywhere. It looked and sounded like World War Three had erupted. At first, we thought the river support base, where we'd just been briefed, was under attack.

Then our radios went absolutely crazy: "Scramble the Seawolves! Scramble the Seawolves!" The crew at the compound heard and saw the same commotion, and came racing down in a jeep.

Door gunners sprinted to the helicopters, untied their rotor blades and flipped the firing pins on each rocket. The two AHACs and trail-aircraft co-pilot ran to their helos, threw on chicken-plate armor, jumped aboard, and fired up the engine. As lead copilot, I immediately radioed the Command Post, listened to a situation report and scribbled down mission info—name of the unit in trouble; its radio frequency and call sign; reason for our being scrambled; coordinates of the target; any friendly casualties; from where the in-trouble unit was taking fire, and other information that would help get us on-target, when we arrived overhead.

The two-ship Fire Team lifted off as I donned my own chicken plate and strapped-in. I gave the flight a bearing, then called the local Army sector to see whether artillery was being fired, where shells were landing and their arc, so we could fly underneath them and stay away from impact areas. Good; no action. Tonight, we didn't have to worry about friendly artillery, just the enemy.

I quickly briefed both aircraft crews about the situation and discussed tactics, before we reached the target. I used a folding map illuminated by the UH-1B's red night light and my red-lens flashlight to navigate. Because we were operating under Visual Flight Rules (VFR), we had to see the ground to know where we were. There were no NAVAIDS and very few lights or villages in the area. At least it wasn't raining, which would have forced us to fly on instruments. And it wasn't too difficult to find the fight; we could see plenty of tracers and explosions. Still, it was damned dark!

Word came that a Navy PBR had been hit during night operations, and we were seeing a firefight between the riverboat and VC on the shoreline. The boat's rudder had been blown off, forcing the crew to ram into the river bank. The boat was stuck, taking fire and unable to back off. Our job: Help those boat guys stay alive.

The Navy crew told us where to shoot, and my pilot, Lieutenant LE [name withheld intentionally], rolled in for the first attack run. At that point, all incoming fire hitting the PBR was coming from the river's eastern shoreline. The river made a very pronounced U-turn right there, creating a sort of peninsula in the middle. Horseshoe-shaped, the river was on both sides of our flight track.

And right smack in the middle, Hell was waiting for us. We were flying into a trap the VC and NVA had set up to shoot down Seawolves. Turns out that the enemy was pissed, thanks to our success in the Moc Hoa area disrupting the flow of troops into South Vietnam. The bad guys knew Seawolves would come running to protect PBRs in trouble. They counted on it—and we did exactly that. Special Forces guys later found intel confirming that an ambush had been set up specifically to draw in Seawolf helos and shoot them down.

When LE pushed over from 800 feet and started firing rockets from about 600 feet, the freakin' world opened up on us. The VC had positioned that captured Armored Personnel Carrier (APC) and its minigun right in the middle of the river's horseshoe. They were firing that minigun directly at us—up to 6,000 rounds of 7.62 ammunition per minute. Then Chinese .51-caliber machine guns joined in—one on the left bank of the peninsula and one on the right bank. Those shells looked like flaming basketballs coming right at us. We were completely enveloped in enemy tracers—every fifth round being fired. We, the lead helicopter crew, were flying into a wall of fire and lead. The trail ship lost sight of us as we disappeared into a storm of red and green tracers engulfing our rotorcraft. They knew we had been shot down.

My fire team leader-pilot panicked. Somewhere between 300 and 400 feet AGL, LE banked hard left, breaking off the rocket run—and literally rolled us upside down. Huey helicopters don't fly upside down! We later confirmed being inverted, because an enemy round had gone through the rotor blade—into the top and out the bottom. We were definitely inverted, when that slug hit the blade.

Immediately, our bird went into blade stall. A stall-warning horn blared in our headsets. The red low-RPM warning light flashed. We were falling out of the sky. I remember turning my head and looking over my left shoulder at trees above me. I glanced at the altimeter as we dropped through 40 feet AGL, about to impact the ground at 80-90 knots.

I threw my right arm across the center console, and hit LE on his left shoulder. Hard. That's one way you tell the other pilot you're assuming command of the aircraft. I yelled, "I've got it!" And that's the last thing I remember. Training and rote memory muscle took over. Next thing I knew, we were flying straight and level at 1,000 feet, about a half-mile away from the action. Alive.

The right door gunner (Bob Beckes) said he heard someone screaming, when we went into blade stall. He was leaning over and unable to sit up, because he was pressed against the back bulkhead. He believed we were going straight into the ground. He recalled seeing our helo skids barely clearing stalks in a rice paddy, and noting that the outside air was damned hot.

The crew chief (Chief Coldsnow) and door gunner directly behind me said I'd grabbed the controls, rolled the aircraft to a level attitude, lowered the collective to regain rotor RPM (and to shut off the alarm, I suspect), and kept us from slamming into the trees or rice paddy.

To this day, I'm convinced that The Hand of God saved us.

Although well away from the battle, I was scared shitless, breathing heavily and wondering how the hell we'd survived that run. All I remembered was seeing a firehose of red tracers and flaming red basketballs coming at us from all sides. Our trail ship then flew alongside and exclaimed that they couldn't believe we were still alive. LE was stunned and silent. He didn't say a word.

Radios were blaring, saying the PBR guys were still rammed into the river bank, unable to move, still taking fire. We had to go back. Make more attack runs. LE didn't want to go. The door gunners and I said we had to return. We just couldn't let those sailors get shot up and killed. So, we went back. It was the hardest thing I ever did in my life—consciously decide to go back into that ferocious Hell-storm again, knowing the bad guys had unbelievable firepower. And knowing our chances of survival were mighty damn slim.

Shifting our inbound line, we made a couple more firing runs. After expending all our ordnance (rockets and minigun/door gunner ammo), we flew to the Moc Hoa airstrip to refuel and rearm. I don't recall how many times we flew back into the battle that night. Then a miracle happened! A pair of U.S. Navy VAL-4 OV-10 Black Ponies heard our radio comms and flew over to lend a hand. They carried 20-mm cannons and Zuni rockets, considerably heavier firepower than we had, but less of it. They attacked and immediately shut down that APC and minigun.

Special Forces guys on the ground reported a bunch of VC running through an open field to the West. We diverted to the area and turned on our landing lights. Hundreds of VC and NVA soldiers were running for a wood line and cover. We opened up with rockets, miniguns and door guns, again exhausting our ammo. The Black Ponies also joined in, making a few strafing runs with 20-mm cannon. Roughly a hundred enemy combatants were killed.

The stuck-PBR guys held their position against the river bank until daylight, when another PBR arrived and pulled them free. Incredibly, no U.S. military personnel died that night. Very grateful PBR crewmen said we saved their lives. I felt the OV-10 Black Ponies saved ours.

I said the rosary every day for the rest of my tour, and I thanked Almighty God for sparing me that night. I still do, fifty-some years later.

Back at Ben Luc, nobody wanted to talk about the battle we'd just survived. We seemed to be shell-shocked. I didn't even log the night's horror in my diary, because I was too emotionally rattled. I remember thinking, "I don't have to write this one down. It's burned into my memory forever."

Epilogue: I later took a Huey down to Binh Thuy, our headquarters, to get certified as a test pilot for our detachment. I was assigned a bunk in an open bay with other bunk beds. Showers were a luxury, since we didn't have real showers at our Det. The VAL-4 Black Ponies were based at Binh Thuy's cushy headquarters. Typical fixed-wing jerks, they thought they were superior to helicopter pilots. While I was in the shower, one of those Black Pony drivers came in, telling a buddy about this firefight they'd gotten into up in Moc Hoa. I knew he was one of the pilots who'd saved my life. But the guy was such a braggart that I couldn't bring myself to thank him. I think about that sometimes and wonder whether I should have spoken up. But honestly, he was such a dork that I simply couldn't give him the satisfaction of saving a bunch of helo pilots' butts.

Flying a Navy UH-1B "Huey," Sam Feola (Seawolf 78) served as an Attack Helicopter Aircraft Commander and Fire Team Leader in Helicopter Attack (Light) Squadron Three, during his one-year combat tour. The HA(L)-3 Seawolves were the most decorated Navy squadron in the Vietnam War and in Naval Aviation History. Sam logged 820 flight hours on 524 combat missions, 291 at night. He earned the Distinguished Flying Cross for Heroism, two Single Action Air Medals, 18 strike/flight air medals, the Vietnamese Cross of Gallantry with Silver Star and several Vietnam campaign and service medals. He also received a Presidential Unit Citation and Meritorious Service Medal. Feola later flew the carrier-based anti-submarine warfare SH-3D, and conducted drone-recovery missions at the Pacific Missile Test Center in California, flying the SH-3D, CH-3E, and CH-46D. He received a Sikorski Rescue Citation for saving a Marine jet pilot, who had ejected over the ocean, and a Boeing Rescue Citation for retrieving a *civilian vehicle crash victim in steep mountainous terrain. He concluded 11 years of Navy active duty as VXE-6 Helicopter Operations Officer, flying the twin-engine UH-1N, supporting scientists in Antarctica. He then worked for a civilian contractor in Antarctica, Hawaii, the Marshall Islands and Turkey. As President of a joint Canadian-American company, Sam supported Canadian troops in Bosnia and Afghanistan. He later served as a Raytheon Program Director, managing the company's $1.2 billion U.S. Antarctic program and overseeing construction of the new South Pole Station. Ultimately, he devoted 20 years to the Antarctic program. The U.S. Geological Survey honored Sam's service as a Navy helicopter pilot and commercial contractor for the National Science Foundation's U.S. Antarctic Program by designating an Antarctic feature "Mount Feola."*

HELL HITS THE INDEPENDENCE
Robert F. Klotz

At dawn on a December day in 1965, the USS Independence, the first Atlantic Fleet aircraft carrier to see combat in Vietnam, was steaming homeward off the U.S. East Coast. The aircraft of Air Wing Seven were poised for a mass "fly off," its aviators anxious to launch. A big welcoming ceremony awaited us at Naval Air Station (NAS) Oceana, Virginia.

Fighter Squadron 41's commanding officer (CO), Commander Bob "Big Daddy" Gormley—our Skipper—and his radar intercept officer (RIO), "Wild Bill" Cody, eased their F-4 Phantom II into position on the outboard waist catapult. Following a couple of A-4 Skyhawks now waiting on the two bow cats, they'd be the first of several F-4s to launch. Wild Bill was holding the CO's dress blue uniform in his lap, because there was no place to stow it in the fighter's cockpit. Gormley would need it for the ceremonies ashore. Medals and ribbons befitting his rank and combat experience had been carefully positioned. Wild Bill was to make sure the jacket and its imposing array would not be disturbed during the cat launch and short flight to NAS Oceana.

A few feet from Gormley and Wild Bill, Lieutenant Commander "Wink" Winkowski and his RIO sat on the inboard waist cat, their F-4 also ready to launch.

Today, I was the RIO for Lieutenant Tom Sanders in another Phantom II. As the third F-4 in the launch sequence, we were parked behind and perpendicular to the Skipper's fighter, positioned to make a hard left turn and taxi onto that catapult, following the Skipper. I could look to our left and see his F-4's afterburners. However, we were sheltered by the outboard cat's Jet Blast Deflector (JBD), a hinged barrier raised at an angle to protect other aircraft and deck personnel from jet exhaust, during launches.

I decided to snap some action photos from directly behind the Skipper's Phantom as it took a cat shot. "Coming home" launch pictures would make an ideal wrap-up to my combat-photo journal. To frame the shot perfectly, I raised my helmet's visor, dropped the oxygen mask to one side and held the viewfinder of a spanking-new 35-mm camera up to my eye. Thunderous noise and heat boiled up and over the JBD as the Skipper's F-4 went into full afterburner prior to launch. The hulking, heavy jet squatted as the cat fired, thrust flinging the Phantom II forward.

A U.S. Navy VF-41 F-4B Phantom II launches, as an A-4 Skyhawk strike force maneuvers into position.

Then Hell hit the Independence.

Where the Phantom had filled my viewfinder a heartbeat ago, a huge fireball erupted. It was so massive I thought the fighter had exploded on the catapult. I don't remember dropping the camera, but I do recall reaching for the canopy-unlatch switch. I wanted out! With that fireball coming at us, my precise thought was: "I'm going to be roasted!"

Instinct screamed, "GET OUT!" But training said, "STAY!" I had a better chance of surviving—at least for now—if I stayed in the airplane. As fast as my finger had leaped to the canopy-open switch, it now reversed direction. I slapped my mask back on, ensuring life-giving oxygen was flowing, then snapped my visor down for additional protection.

The fireball and blast wave from the outboard waist catapult expanded and passed over us. Both of our canopies held. Tiny heat fractures or "crazing" appeared, but the structure was intact.

I don't remember Tom or me saying anything. We just stared at our mirrors, and stayed off the radio. For now, we were safe.

Seconds later, we knew a disaster had erupted around our fighter. The command-chain radios exploded in emergency chatter: "Fire! Fire! Fire! Fire on the flight deck!"

Then, "Eject! Eject! Eject!" followed immediately by: "I see one good chute!"

All hands immediately responded. Looking to my left, through the residual fire and boiling smoke, I saw that the Skipper's Phantom was gone. I didn't know where it was, but someone evidently had ejected from something. For all I knew, the fighter was in pieces, scattered across the catapult and deck.

I was absolutely stunned to see a member of the launch crew appear from behind the JBD, rubbing his eyes. He was naked, his clothes burned off. Only his belt and dungarees' belt loops remained, still on fire. We heard later that the crewman had saved most of his money during our cruise, and all that cash—carried in a wallet—was lost when his clothes burned. He ultimately recovered from his burns, and somehow recouped all but $25 of his hoard.

Then, one of the most skillful displays of flying proficiency I was ever privileged to witness manifested. Through the chaotic radio communications, Skipper Gormley's voice calmly emerged.

"Uh, this is Alpha Golf One-Oh-One—Big Daddy. I'm airborne at three miles, dead ahead, straight and level at angels two. My RIO's punched out, but I don't seem to have any indications of fire right now. Tower, could you direct somebody over to me? Have them look me over? And pick up my RIO…and give me his status. Over."

Outstanding! Gormley was airborne and, at least for now, still flying! He had disregarded all the ship's frantic radio calls, simply concentrating on the cat launch and the business of flying his airplane. Even Wild Bill's ejection gave the Skipper one less thing to worry about, in case things went south in a hurry— which they still could.

Wild Bill hadn't waited to clarify where those triple ejection commands had originated. The "Eject!" command in his helmet's earphones had been enough for him to pull the yellow-and-black ejection rings. He wasn't about to be left behind, maybe to die alone in the next few seconds.

A RIO ejecting from the back seat of an F-4 always runs the risk of a hazard known as "Martin-Baker Back"—a compression fracture of one's lower lumbar vertebrae. It's caused by a cannon shell firing, which propels the Martin-Baker ejection seat up and out of the aircraft. That's why the Skipper, worried about Bill, had requested an immediate rescue. F-4 backseaters are more prone to suffering the temporarily incapacitating—and painful—back injury, because a RIO must brace himself against the aft cockpit's fixed, flat floorboards. A pilot can stretch his legs out, bracing his feet against adjustable rudder pedals, a better body position for ejection.

An A-4 pilot scooted over in a flash to check the commander's damaged F-4.

"Skipper, you have a badly collapsed belly fuel tank. Its nose cone is crushed. The tail cone is gone, and the tank is empty. You have some badly singed 'tail feathers,' but no fire, no other damage and no leaks."

Gormley acknowledged his thanks. Ultimately, we'd learn that, unbeknownst to the Skipper and others, his Phantom's jettisonable belly tank had carried a partial fuel load. Why? Possibly a fueling error. Regardless, that's the worst possible external fuel tank condition for a catapult launch. The tank must be completely full or completely empty.

As the Skipper's F-4 was subjected to the catapult shot's rapid acceleration, the belly tank's partial fuel load was transformed into an aft-moving hydraulic ram, sucking the nose cone inward, blowing the tail cone off and dumping jet fuel. That fuel, splashed along the catapult track's full length, was ignited by the twin J79 engines' afterburners. An explosion drove jet fuel-fed fire into the catapult spaces below deck, burning and injuring many more of the crew.

Adding to the mayhem, deck crewmen were blown overboard. Several men dived off the port side, aiming for uptilted safety netting that ringed the carrier. From there, they could work their way to safety under the flight deck. But some received an unexpected, blast-assisted velocity boost (as if adrenaline wasn't enough), causing them to overshoot the netting and fall to the water some 70 ft. below.

Always-ready recovery teams eventually rescued all those in the water, including Bill, the Skipper's RIO. Given the circumstances, Gormley couldn't fault Wild Bill's decision to eject. But the Skipper's dress blues were lost, a casualty that turned Big Daddy into one P.O.'ed CO.

During the melee on deck, Winkowski's now completely fire-blackened F-4—still sitting on the inboard cat—finally stirred. In surreal unison, its two now-jet-black canopies "peeked" open about an inch, then closed. Again, they cracked open for a brief second, then closed. It was weird, watching this strange dance-of-the-canopies. It demonstrated good discipline though. Unable to see outside, Wink, a Navy Test Pilot School graduate, and his RIO were testing the outside environment. Finally, both canopies opened fully and the crewmen exited at a run. Their feet hardly touched the deck until they were inside the ship's island.

Wink's F-4 was later declared a "strike"—damaged beyond repair—but it had saved the crew's tails.

Meanwhile, the Skipper, now alone and flying a "convertible" (a fighter missing one or both canopies) with its backseat ejection rail extended well above the fuselage, really didn't want to be part of the Air Wing's formation flight to the beach. He requested and received permission from CAG, the carrier's Air Wing Commander, to proceed as a solo flight to the naval air station.

Because several press reporters were on board the carrier, word of the fire, as well as rumors about an ejection, had raced ahead.

At the sight of Gormley's empty aft cockpit, Wild Bill's fiancee promptly fainted.

Back on the Independence, damage control teams finally restored order, and the ship prepared to resume flight ops, using undamaged bow catapults.

Tom, my pilot, said, "Shit, Bob! We can't launch! We have a utility hydraulic failure." Damn! Disappointment City. No hydraulics meant no flight control systems, and that meant no launch. Period. Worse, we'd have to go back and face those junior officers. We'd ragged on them earlier, because they didn't have a ride ashore, and were stuck on board until the ship pulled into Norfolk the next day. Something about wives and who'd be smiling first....

But this didn't fit the profile of a normal utility hydraulic system failure. Usually, that system failed on startup or after some other physical event. Maybe we just blew a circuit breaker. I started scanning the breaker panel by my knee, searching for one that had popped.

Tom interrupted. "Bob, we just lost the port engine! That fireball must've sucked all the air out of it, 'cause it just unwound. Let's taxi over to the island, see if we can get the engine started, and if so, we'll launch off the bow with the others. Sound good?" With the left engine powered up, we should get our utility hydraulics back.

"Roger that, Tom. Let's get off this #*%! boat, if we can."

We managed to launch and were soon on shore, grinning big. Oh, and the accident review board said the film in my camera was blank. Right!

The late-Robert F. Klotz flew 106 combat missions, logged 300 carrier landings and 1,000 hr. of flight time. Later, he became an "X-Shop" charter member, working on McDonnell Douglas's two YC-15 prototypes, and, in 26 years with NASA's Jet Propulsion Laboratory, was financial manager for the InfraRed Astronomical Satellite and TOPEX/Poseidon projects. He received the NASA Exceptional Service medal prior to his retirement.

FLY HARD, PLAY HARD
Rick Couch

The old adage is true, and those who served in Southeast Asia can attest to that truth: War is hell. As a forward air controller, I flew the OV-10A *Bronco* during the Vietnam War, operating from a base in Thailand. Our squadron lost several great aviators, and each loss was horrific.

For centuries, though, warriors survived battlefield horrors by blowing off steam, whenever possible. Vietnam was no different, particulary for those who fought in the air. With the support of mates and the right attitude, one can survive combat and actually enjoy each flight. Looking back, that year-long combat tour was a memorable mix of airborne adventure and raucous postflight celebration-of-life.

Our unit routinely supported ground troops in Vietnam's I Corps area, the Laos Steel Tiger and Barrell Roll regions, and Cambodia. In Laos, our primary missions were disrupting supplies moving down the Ho Chi Minh Trail and supporting Laotian Army forces in the Plain de Jars. In Cambodia, we supported loyalist troops in various villages around the country. Each of our AORs (Areas of Responsibility) posed vastly different risks.

North American Rockwell OV-10 Bronco
U.S. Air force

The OV-10 was a superb aircraft for the forward air control mission. Its twin turboprop engines provided plenty of power for the typical FAC combat load: a 300-gallon centerline fuel tank, two seven-tube launchers carrying 2.75-inch white phosphorus (WP or "Willy Pete") rockets, and four 7.62-mm machine guns with a total of 2,000 rounds. At night, two pods containing four flares in each were added. Ejection seats were rated from zero-zero (on the ground, with zero airspeed) up to the aircraft's maximum speed. In every case that I know, those ejection seats worked flawlessly; none failed.

Generally, we flew the two-seat *Bronco* solo. However, a variant of the OV-10, designated Pave Nail, operated with a back-seater we called a Sewer Pipe Operator. Pave Nail SPOs aimed a targeting pod and laser designator—mounted under the aircraft fuselage—with a sighting system that resembled a sewer pipe.

On occasion, Marines flew in our back seats to coordinate naval gun fire from offshore ships in the Gulf of Tonkin. Once we located viable targets, we'd typically call in bomb-laden fighters, then fire white phosphorus rockets to identify areas they were to attack. We often directed both tactical aircraft and naval gunfire at the same time.

R.A. Hill, U.S. Navy

One memorable mission took place in I Corps, north of the Cua Viet River and just south of the DMZ (Demilitarized Zone). This was a high-threat area for OV-10s, which operated at relatively low altitudes. During the pre-mission intelligence briefing, I was warned that 23-mm, 57-mm, and 85-mm antiaircraft artillery (triple-A) emplacements were all over that area. The most dangerous threat, though, were man-portable, shoulder-fired SA-7 *Grail* surface-to-air missiles. That tidbit got my attention. On a previous mission over there, I'd narrowly avoided one of those damned SA-7s.

Around that time, we lost three aircraft in the span of 36 hours. I remember preflighting my OV-10 and wondering whether I'd come back from that mission. *Is this my time?* You never knew. After takeoff, though, I focused on flying, not dying.

Onsite, the Tactical Air Command Post (TACP)—call sign "Big"—called for a standard visual reconnaissance, and I started hunting for southbound troops or materiel movements. I soon spotted what appeared to be troops in an old fire base, and reported that these were targets worth striking. An airborne command and control crew immediately sent a flight of two F-4 Phantoms to hammer the bad guys. Just as the F-4s checked in, my right engine failed and its prop auto-feathered. I moved the prop-control lever to "Unfeather", but nothing happened. In the feathered or low-drag position—prop blades edge-on to the direction of airflow—an engine restart was impossible.

Normally, losing an engine wasn't a big deal for the twin-engine OV-10. I still had one motor keeping me airborne. I reported to "Big" that I had an emergency, was headed for the water, and planned to land at Da Nang. I immediately got a call from "King", an Airborne Command and Control aircraft that handled rescues, asking whether I needed help. At the time, I didn't think so. That situation was about to change.

Hearing that I had a problem, one of my squadron-mates flew over and joined on my wing. My one-engine *Bronco* was still carrying high-drag external stores, which translated to a slow descent toward the water. I couldn't maintain altitude on one engine. First order of business was to jettison the center line fuel tank and targeting pods to decrease drag.

I hit the Emergency Jettison button—and nothing happened. My wingman reported all stores were still attached. So, I selected a setting that should jettison each store separately, mashed the pickle button and…nothing. All stores failed to release. The water was coming up smartly. If I couldn't get rid of those draggy external stores, I'd have to eject. And soon.

My astute wingman suggested pressing *and holding* the Emergency Jettison button. I did, and those stubborn stores immediately separated. *Free at last!* About 1,500 feet above the water, I now had enough power to climb back to a respectable altitude and land at Da Nang without further incident. Turns out that an engine fuel pump had failed, ensuring I never would have gotten that engine restarted.

After demanding combat missions, aircrews were ready for a stiff drink and some serious decompression. Our remarkably close-knit squadron was known for working hard and partying harder. A favorite sport was "carrier landings." Pilots at Nakhon Phanom (NKP) had a table built specifically for that purpose—about 20 feet long, a couple of feet above the ground and covered with a plastic sheet. Lubricated liberally with soap and a bit of water, that table was a perfect platform for "carrier landings." Get a run at it, dive head-first, and sliiiiide.

Rick demonstrates improper carrier-landing form, missing the "cable" held by 'mates.

Carrier landings are risky, as any naval aviator will attest. Slightly inebriated Air Force pilots didn't always nail the proper glide slope on approach. At one particularly great Fourth of July party, several guys crashed into the approach end of our makeshift carrier "deck." At least six intrepid pilots subsequently were grounded due to injuries, prompting the squadron commander to prohibit carrier landings for a month.

Fortunately, the ban was lifted before the Marine Corps birthday, which was an ideal excuse for a massive celebration. The Da Nang officer club's entire floor was converted to a carrier deck. Lubed with water and soap, the floor avoided that deadly "approach end" danger posed by our low-altitude table. In turn, we'd run at full speed, dive belly-down and slide for record-setting distance. One over-exuberant Marine made a hard landing, bashed his forehead and opened a huge gash. Not to worry, 'mate!

We tossed him into a jeep and roared off to the hospital. Emergency room nurses were not amused. They threw us out, so back to the club we went. Carrier landings resumed without additional casualties.

As a career-broadening experience, our unit crafted a pilot-exchange program with a Navy A-7 squadron on an aircraft carrier in the Gulf of Tonkin. The navy would send four pilots on a Carrier Onboard Delivery (COD) aircraft to Thailand and fly four of our pilots back to the boat. Watching carrier combat operations was fascinating, and evoked renewed respect for our Navy brethren's flying skills.

Visiting Navy pilots always arrived with flight suit pockets full of American green. We invariably had a poker or 4-5-6 game going in the squadron "party hooch," and our navy compatriots willingly jumped in with both feet. Ah, we did love taking their money.

Navy pilots typically flew with us over Laos to observe how we conducted FAC missions. Being generous sorts, we gave them plenty of stick time in the *Bronco*. Naturally, after these guest-pilot missions, we retired to the bar and traded war stories. The booze flowed freely and a few of our maritime comrades would fade out. On one such occasion, a young Navy lieutenant woke up to discover that he'd broken his ankle. It was now solidly encased in a plaster cast. Shocked, he demanded to know what had happened. In a drunken stuper, he was told, his demonstration of proper carrier-landing technique had gone terribly awry. He'd veered off-course, sailed off the bar and broken his ankle. He recalled absolutely none of that. For three days, he limped around the base with one foot in a cast.

As that lieutenant and his buddies were boarding their COD, en route back to the carrier, the big-foot Navy pilot was worried sick. Without question, the skipper would be furious. Probably throw him in the brig for exercising such poor judgment and breaking an ankle. We pulled one of the lieutenant's buddies aside and let him know there was nothing wrong with that ankle. Once they were back on the carrier, the pilot could remove his cast and jump into an A-7 cockpit.

More than a few enebriated souls were "cast" that year. The base hospital graciously provided the necessary supplies, and its medical staff made sure we were properly trained to cast someone without risking permanent damage to a limb.

The rescue of a shot-down pilot or air crew always dictated a special party, one that included all flying squadrons on the base and a "round robin" visit to each unit's party hooch. On such a night, we returned to our own hooch for one last round and a recap of the day's rescue. Some guy wandered in, sat on the sofa and promptly passed out. We had no idea who he was. We knew most of the crew members on-base, but nobody recognized this character. Aha! Yet another candidate for a "broken" leg. In short order, his entire leg, from hip to toe, was immobilized in a massive cast. Our patient slept through the entire process.

The squadron guest bedroom was vacant, so we carefully tucked the well-casted drunk into bed. About 8 o'clock the next morning, we heard a blood-curdling scream from down the hallway. Our mystery comrade had awakened, obviously wondering what the hell had happened to him. Then silence. Finally, a pilot decided to check on him. The guy was long gone. A horrified hooch maid babbled that our "patient" had removed his cast with a banana knife and escaped.

A couple of days later, one of our guys solved the unknown-drunk mystery. The intrepid patient was in the base exchange, selling encyclopedias.

Rick Couch earned a bachelor degree in Mechanical Engineering from Texas A&M (1968), a masters in Aeronautical Engineering from the Air Force Institute of Technology (1974), and a masters in Systems Management from the University of Southern California (1981). After commissioning, Rick completed pilot training and operational tours in the C-141 and OV-1OA. In

1975, he graduated from the USAF Test Pilot School (USAF TPS) and was assigned to the 4950th Test Wing at Wright-Patterson Air Force Base, Ohio. He flew developmental tests of the C-141 All Weather Landing System, before returning to USAF TPS as an instructor. Following a tour at Headquarters Air Force Systems Command (AFSC), supporting classified flight test activities, he completed a stint at the Industrial College of the Armed Forces, then returned to Edwards AFB to command the new B-2 bomber Combined Test Force (CTF). He stood-up the 1,200-person B-2 CTF, ran initial B-2 flight test operations, and planned overall B-2 flight test and logistics test operations. In 1989, he and Northrop's test pilot, Bruce Hinds, flew the B-2's historical first flight. Rick subsequently served as Vice Commander of the 6510th Test Wing, and in 1990, was named Deputy Director of the Tri-Service Standoff Attack Missile System Program Office.

Rick retired from the Air Force in 1992 and joined Martin Marietta, responsible for National Test Bed integration testing at Falcon Air Force Base, Colorado (now Schriever AFB), in support of the Ballistic Missile Defense Program. He also managed the Lockheed Martin Test and Transition organization for the BellSouth Business Process Reengineering Integration Office in Atlanta, Georgia. In 1997, Rick was assigned to manage Lockheed Martin Information Systems' Fort Worth Operations, overseeing support equipment and training systems design, development and production for the F-16, F-2, C-130, F-117 and F-35 aircraft. In 2005, Rick joined the Lockheed Martin Global Training and Logistics team as a Business Development Manager for air mobility programs supporting opportunities for the C-130, C-130J, C-5, F-16 and F-35 aircrew and associated maintenance training programs. He retired from Lockheed Martin in 2012, and continues to fly as a Mission Pilot and Safety Officer for the Civil Air Patrol. He is a Fellow of the Society of Experimental Test Pilots, a Life member of Daedalians, and a member of the Pioneers of Stealth.

BAILOUT AND RESCUE...AGAIN

John Casper & William B. Scott

As the air war heated up in Vietnam, newly minted fighter pilots were rapidly rushed to Southeast Asia and thrown into combat. Casualty rates were high, because pilots had little "seasoning," before encountering deadly threats—surface-to-air missiles (SAM) and anti-aircraft artillery (AAA).

Then-First Lieutenant John Casper was one of many F-105 Thunderchief pilots that started flying missions as soon as he arrived at Korat air base in Thailand. In the span of a single month, he earned the dubious distinction of being shot down and rescued twice. And yet, he was fortunate. During the roughly six months John was at Korat, his squadron lost 16 aircraft and eight pilots.

This high loss rate was more a reflection of the F-105's inherent characteristics than its pilots' expertise and experience. The F-105 "Thud" had been designed to carry a large nuclear bomb internally, race at speeds topping Mach 2 (twice the speed of sound) into enemy territory, toss the nuke in a loft delivery maneuver and high-tail it back home. Consequently, the Thud didn't turn well and was no match for the enemy's nimble MiG fighters in a traditional high-g, turning "furball" air-to-air engagement.

For conventional warfare in Vietnam, Air Force F-105s were modified to carry a large fuel tank in the bomb bay and a variety of underwing stores, ranging from eight 750-pound bombs to a pair of 3,000-pounders packed with high explosives. Extra fuel tanks, electronic jamming pods and 1,000-pound or 2,000-pound bombs also were routinely carried on wing stations. The Thud's single turbojet engine produced about 17,000 pounds of thrust in military power and 22,000 pounds in afterburner. Still, heavily loaded F-105s needed water injection to get an extra 2,600-pound boost on takeoff.

"We operated from an 8,000-foot runway [at Korat] and you were just about in the overrun, when you rotated," John said.

Initially, he flew attack missions in southeast North Vietnam, a region supposedly less dangerous than "up north" around Hanoi. Not so. On his eighth mission (8 August 1966), John was shot down during a Mu Gia Pass mission in Route Pack 1, an area north of the Demilitarized Zone. It was his second week in Southeast Asia.

U.S. Air Force

Welcome to the war.

John was Number Four in a flight of four Thuds, each carrying 750-pound bombs. Because a thick overcast obscured their assigned or "fragged" target, Lead headed for the alternate, a batch of caves concealing 37-mm guns. Soon, four pilots were sequentially trying to fling a single bomb into those caverns.

"As I came off-target, I heard a solid 'thump' and all the cockpit lights came on. Flames were streaming behind me, and 20-30 seconds later, I lost hydraulics. Then the airplane pitched over [nose down]." Having lost control, John ejected at around 8,000 feet.

High-stress situations typically trigger a phenomenon called time dilation. Everything seems to happen in slow motion, and one's mind tends to focus on the trivial. Maybe it's a protective technique, when a life-threatening situation overwhelms the wetware between our ears. As the canopy flew off, John's slow-motion awareness locked onto "the great visibility. I could really see without that canopy!"

His parachute opened as advertised, and he plunged into thick trees along a karst ridge. The chute caught, leaving John hanging 10 feet above a relatively clear forest floor. Then something broke loose, dumping him on the ground. "Somehow, I bit my tongue, so now I'm all bloody," but otherwise unhurt.

Activating his survival radio, he reported being down and in one piece. The other three F-105s had to hit a tanker, but Lead said they'd be back. Meanwhile, "hide and call back in an hour." John found a sizable brush pile and crawled in. Well concealed, "I wondered about snakes in there," but they were a lesser concern than voices he was hearing nearby. "I pulled out my trusty thirty-eight revolver and thought, 'This isn't good.'"

By mid-to-late afternoon, his Thud flight was back on-scene, reporting that a team of A-1 "Spads" and a Jolly Green rescue helicopter were on their way. The flight lead had pinpointed his downed pilot's location and directed the rescue force to it by making a low pass overhead. Following radioed directions, a helo soon hovered directly over John. The Jolly Green crew couldn't see him, but John hollered, "Just lower the penetrator!"

A metal tree penetrator descended through the foliage, its petal-like seats folded up. "And the [excited] lieutenant did exactly what you're taught not to do," John admitted. "I grabbed the penetrator, before it touched the ground, and [its static electric charge] knocked me on my ass." Metal penetrators dragged through the air naturally build up a static charge capable of killing a guy. All aircrews are instructed to ensure a penetrator hits the dirt and discharges, before grabbing it.

Shocked but not injured, John rotated a seat "petal" down, jumped astride the penetrator and cleared the helo winch operator to haul him up. The Jolly Green suddenly developed an engine problem that dictated "leaving the hover" and flying forward, before John could be winched aboard. Consequently, he was dragged through the tree tops, getting thoroughly beaten up, but managed to hang on. Finally hauled into the rotorcraft, John tried to hug everybody, until a crew chief strapped down his grateful, scratched and bloody passenger to keep him from falling out. Minutes later, John was dropped off at NKP (Nakhon Phanom) where OV-10 FAC pilots promptly dragged him to the bar and a celebration.

Bleeding from cuts and scratches, John eventually was patched up by a flight surgeon and declared fit to fly. A C-130 ferried him to Korat the next morning, and he was back in a Thud the following day. Commanders, at the time, were firm believers in an old cowboy truism: Get bucked off, and you get right back on the horse, before you have time to think about aches and pains. John's next bombing mission was in the same area he'd just narrowly escaped.

On 14 September 1966, John strapped in for his 28th combat mission and launched with six 750-pound bombs onboard. He again was Number Four in a four-ship of F-105s fragged to attack a railroad bridge northeast of Hanoi.

"We flew directly across Hanoi at about 500 knots in a spread formation.

Started climbing, and just before we rolled in, they fired three SAMs right up through the middle of our flight," John vividly recalls. "I'd never seen a SAM that close. Not like you could reach out and touch 'em."

To dodge the missiles, three F-105s broke into the target, dropped their bombs and took off. John broke the other direction, away from the target. "I came up and didn't see [the other Thuds]. The sky was empty; no flak or anything. It was surreal. [But] there was the bridge, so I rolled in and dropped, looked back and saw the the span drop into the river."

Feeling good, John then discovered why no AAA or missiles filled the sky. A MiG-17 fighter was directly abeam, homing on his F-105 and closing rapidly.

"He was shooting at me; I could see the gun flashes. I started to turn, and with only about 400 knots, I thought, 'This isn't going to work very well'. But we'd been taught what's called a high-g roll underneath—basically a snap-roll. So, I snapped the throttle to idle, put the speed brakes out, pulled the stick into my lap and gave it all the rudder I could. I have no idea what gyrations the airplane went through, but I came out pointed straight down with maybe 150 knots of airspeed. And no MiG-17. He must have thought he'd gotten me."

Alone and clearly vulnerable, John reported "off the target," lit the afterburner and headed east, toward the coast of North Vietnam. The other fighters in his flight were 20 miles away, but turned "to come get me. But I'm going out, they're coming at me—and we miss each other." Once that was sorted out, the other three Thuds reversed course and started chasing their lost-lieutenant wingman.

"I said, I'll meet you over the water." But the enemy kept dogging him. "I saw a glint of sunlight and here comes a MiG-21. ...I turned into him, but after about 90 degrees [of turn], I said, 'This isn't going to work very well, either!' So, I lit the burner and dove for the dirt. That's when I saw 820 knots indicated [airspeed]—Mach 1.2-plus—to get down on the deck."

Unable to catch a supersonic Thud, the MiG gave up. "The F-105 eats an enormous amount of gas in afterburner," John explained. "I could see the coastline, so pulled it out of burner and started a climb. But crossing a ridge line, all hell broke loose. A chunk of my wing came off, fire lights came on... I kinda knew I'd been hit," he deadpans.

One of the trailing pilots called a missile launch, just as John pulled up. Lead corrected, "No, that's four. He's hit." A 57-mm anti-aircraft gun had nailed the jet, blowing off a section of its wing.

"They later said I was a huge ball of fire. But now I could see the water," John said. At the time, 95 percent of pilots who made it to the ocean, before ejecting, were picked up. But 95 percent of those who punched out over land were not rescued.

USAF F-105 shot down over North Vietnam
blog.daum.net

Even though badly damaged, John's Thud was still flying and had hydraulic power. Maybe the air-driven RAT (ram air turbine) had deployed and was delivering emergency electrical and hydraulic power. For whatever reason, "I had good control and could fly the airplane for awhile. I picked up a glide of about 250 knots and glanced at my mirrors.

"You know why they put mirrors in jet fighters, right?" John grins. "It's so you can look at yourself and say, 'Damn! Am I cool!' That's about all they're good for. But in my mirrors, I could see [flames] from the wing root aft. And I had fire in the cockpit, when I finally [ejected]."

Without question, he stayed with the crippled Thud far too long. John should have ejected around 2,000 feet above the water, but delayed until roughly 300 feet. "I was right on the edge of everything. I must have keyed the mic somewhere in there, because the last thing [my flight] heard me say was, 'Jesus! Look at all the fucking boats down there!' And they weren't ours."

But the ghost of Murphy—that sage who observed, "Anything that can go wrong will go wrong, and at the worst possible time"—was still riding on John's shoulder. For the second time in a month, the pilot raised his Thud's ejection handles to blow the canopy off. This time, it didn't depart.

Fortunately, the Thud's ballistic-type ejection seat was built with a pointed canopy breaker mounted atop its structure. John squeezed trigger-like handles, blasted through the canopy and started tumbling. He opened his eyes and "saw all the [parachute] risers come right up between my legs in front of me. I hit the water shortly thereafter," entangled in a web of rope-like nylon risers.

His flight mates thought he'd gone in. "No chute. No beeper." Low on fuel, the other three Thud pilots marked the area and headed for a tanker, planning to get a search-and-rescue effort launched. Then they heard a faint beeper, a distress signal from an emergency radio. John was alive.

"I hit the water and went down like a stone," he recalled. "I didn't have the water wings deployed, I was still tied to the seat pan" and was wrapped in risers. "I [pulled] my knife and started sawing on risers to get a hand free and deploy a water wing. I looked up, saw the sun reflecting off the water... and remember thinking, 'Oh man; I'm going to drown out here. And that's just not right!'"

He finally inflated a water wing, popped to the surface, sawed himself free of those risers, and scrambled into a one-man life raft. Fortunately, a thoroughly soaked survival radio operated as designed. "Without that radio, you're not going to be rescued," he declared.

Because "I'd landed in the middle of a major shipping lane between China and North Vietnam," fishing boats, junks and anything else that would float were immediately pursuing him. "I thought I was near Haiphong, but was waaaay north of that." He had splashed down about 20 miles south of China's border, so far north that Navy search and rescue crews had no navigation charts of that area. Further, a series of islands along that route were heavily defended.

"I had no idea how much time had passed, but heard some gunfire and a Navy A-1 [Spad] flew right over me." John radioed that the Spad had just passed overhead, and there were two massive junks with raised sails about a quarter mile from his position. "I said, 'There's a guy in the bow [of a junk] and I think he's shooting at me.' The Navy guy said, 'I don't see you, but I see the junk.' He rolled in and fired several of those big Zuni rockets—and the junk just disappeared. There was crap flying everywhere. All the little boats [instantly] turned around and parked."

John reported seeing considerable gunfire on a nearby island. The A-1 pilot responded, "Have you noticed those geysers in the water from time to time?" Yes, he had. "Well, they're using you for mortar practice!"

A concerted recovery effort was underway, but was running into trouble. An Air Force twin-engine Grumman HU-16 Albatross "flying boat" made a rescue attempt, but came under blistering enemy fire and lost an engine. One crew member also was wounded, forcing the Albatross to head for a safe haven. As dusk approached, the entire rescue force consisted of two Navy A-1s and an inbound Navy/Sikorsky CH-3 Sea King helicopter. John later learned that a Navy crew from Helicopter Squadron 6, the "Raunchy Redskins," had taken a vote, before committing to go after the downed Air Force pilot floating in dangerous waters a few miles from China. Two gutsy officers and two enlisted airmen gave a thumbs-up and launched.

Following a tortuous route that threaded islands bristling with enemy guns and troops, the Sea King relied on a direction finder (DF) monitoring *Guard* frequency to home on John's position. When the big bird finally flew over, reversed course and came to a hover, the lieutenant was ecstatic. "I'm gonna get out of here!" The crew lowered a rescue 'horse collar' and John slipped it over his head and shoulders. As the hoist started pulling him up, the exhausted pilot fell out. The helicopter circled back and again hovered overhead, but rotor downwash pushed John under the aircraft.

Eventually, he managed to get back into the horse collar—and "the hoist shorts out. I'm [suspended] about a hundred feet below the helicopter and *now it's time to leave!* These guys have had about all the fun they can stand." As the big chopper maneuvered to get the hell out of there, John swung well below the fuselage, until the balky winch was back in business.

The rescue H-3 was under fire for 35-40 minutes, during which its two gunners fired more than 3,000 rounds. Meanwhile, the pair of Navy A-1 Spads continuously rolled in and fired or dropped ordnance to suppress enemy ground fire.

Finally hauled aboard, John again became a problem, "because I'm trying to hug everybody. They finally let me shoot one of the [side-window] guns, just to settle me down, then strapped me to the floor so I wouldn't fall out" as the pilots dodged incessant streams of anti-aircraft fire. "One of the gunners took time to hand me a little bottle of whiskey—one of those little airline bottles. They all carry [them]. [The USAF rescue crew also] gave me one, when I was shot down the first time." Greatly appreciated, the shot of whiskey was promptly consumed.

Once the Sea King cleared hostile islands, the A-1s returned to their carrier. The helicopter crew, in serious need of fuel, diverted to its destroyer. Hovering just above the deck, the H-3 refueling process "was the damndest thing I'd ever seen," John said. A crew member accepted a hose and nozzle, plugged it into a receptacle and started "passing gas." The helicopter pilots deftly eased their hulking rotorcraft sideways and dipped below the destroyer's deck level. Gravity-fed, fuel flowed at a higher rate, minimizing refueling time.

Soon, the H-3 was off to the carrier USS Constellation, where John was delivered to a helmet-and-goggles-clad deck hand. "All the deck lights go on...and a band [starts] playing the *Star Spangled Banner*! It's surreal! Out of the dark comes this guy, who sticks out his hand and says, 'Welcome back to the states, son. My name's Sharp.' It was four-star Admiral [Ulysses S. Grant] Sharp who happened to be visiting the boat." At the time, Sharp was commander of U.S. forces in the Pacific.

The admiral asked John if he wanted anything. "Well, sir, I'm pretty tired," the pilot admitted. "Could I get a beer and a hamburger? They took me to a private room.... Pretty soon, there's a knock at the door and there's a [steward] with a change of clothes—and a hamburger and a beer." Later, John's washed flight suit and well-cleaned .38 revolver were returned to him.

The deeply appreciative Thud pilot then was spirited from ship-to-ship. "For three days, I was [the admiral's] Air Force showpiece as we went from carrier to carrier. Finally, I told the admiral, 'Sir, I really want to get back to my unit over in Thailand.' He said, 'Oh, we'll get you there.'" Soon, John was aboard an S-2 COD (carrier on delivery) aircraft, catapulted off the ship and ferried to Da Nang air base. With no identification, no name tags on his flight suit and no money, he walked into base operations and announced that he needed to get to Korat, Thailand.

A skeptical, rule-following clerk demanded to see some ID and orders. John's patience meter finally pegged. "Look, I got shot down three days ago and the Navy dropped me off here." Unbeknownst to the wayward lieutenant, Navy personnel had notified a local wing commander that John was inbound, but word hadn't filtered down; nobody at base ops knew when the pilot was arriving. "I'm getting upset," he recalled, "and I touched my gun. Now nobody's happy with me!"

John asked if he could talk to the wing commander, who proceeded to enlighten the base ops clerk. "All I heard was, 'Yes, sir! Yes, sir!' then 'Hey!

Hold that C-130 at the end of the runway!' The one-thirty turned around, picked me up and took me back to my base."

Ultimately, a Navy RA-5C Vigilante photographed the bridge John and his flight had attacked, confirming the span had been dropped, as reported.

Next up: A confab with the squadron commander, who informed John that Air Force policy dictated that he was going home. His war was over. Anybody shot down twice was to be shipped back to the States. Despite his heated protests, John was leaving Southeast Asia.

With a grin, the squadron commander neatly silenced his double-lucky Thud pilot. "John, we just can't afford you anymore!"

John Casper spent the next two years as an openly unhappy T-38 flight instructor. He eventually wrangled an assignment back to Vietnam and completed a second combat tour in the F-105. Despite at least one serious inflight emergency, he never ejected from another fighter. Over a 30-year Air Force career, John logged approximately 5,000 hours in the F-105, T-38, F-5, F-4, A-10, F-16 and F-15. His awards and decorations included the Silver Star, Distinguished Flying Cross, two Purple Hearts and 12 Air Medals. A full second career was with UPS, flying the Douglas DC-8 and Boeing 747.

RESCUE THE RESCUERS

Jim Brennan & William B. Scott

Kaman UH-2A "Clementine"

Air combat in Vietnam was a stew of myriad experiences, ranging from adrenaline-pumping air-to-ground bombing strikes to ferrying troops and equipment into hot landing zones. Rewards and trials were as varied as the missions. Pulling off a target as it vanished in a firestorm of secondary explosions was satisfying payback, after running a gauntlet of gut-wrenching anti-aircraft flak and surface-to-air missile (SAM) threats. Delivering a C-130 load of desperately needed ammunition, food and reinforcements through blistering small arms fire, then taking off and skimming tree tops to ensure wounded soldiers and Marines made it to life-saving field hospitals clearly warranted postflight celebration.

At the bar, though, one fraternity of aviators rarely bought its own drinks—search and rescue (SAR) crews. These were helicopter and fixed-wing pilots, gunners and "swimmers" charged with flying into bad-guy territory and retrieving shot-down pilots and backseaters. Prop-driven Navy and Air Force Douglas A-1 Skyraiders—call sign "Sandy"—armed with rockets, bombs and four 20-mm cannons flew combat SAR to protect helicopter crews, who located, hovered overhead, pulled downed airmen aboard and flew them to safety. Gutsy SAR crews were some of the most highly decorated airmen of the war in Southeast Asia.

August 1967

One of those SAR pilots, Jim Brennan, flew from San Diego to Cubi Point, Philippines, where he joined Helicopter Support Squadron Seven (HC-7), the "Sea Devils." To reduce weight, his Kaman UH-2A's standard flotation gear was removed. Adding two M60 machine guns and armor plating around both pilots' seats prepared the rotorcraft for its SAR role.

After completing survival school, Jim transitioned to Yankee Station off the coast of Vietnam. Typically, the Sea Devils operated from a Navy destroyer in support of both North SAR and South SAR areas. In the latter, UH-2As would launch and orbit, when fighter and attack aircraft—A-4 Skyhawks, F-4 Phantoms, A-6 Intruders and A-7 Corsairs—were flying strike missions.

One of Jim Brennan's more-dicey rescues began on October 3, 1967, an attempted recovery of USAF Major Robert W. Barnett. The F-105 pilot's four-ship "Ozark" flight had departed Korat air base in Thailand to attack a bridge in North Vietnam. When three SA-2 SAMs were launched into the strike force's formation, a warhead detonated behind Barnett's Thud, damaging its hydraulic system and igniting a fire. The pilot tried to make the coastline, but ultimately lost control of the crippled fighter and ejected around 16,000 feet. *

Orbiting over the Gulf of Tonkin, Jim (copilot) and Lieutenant Tim Mclecosky (pilot) were monitoring Ozark flight's radio traffic. Controllers told the UH-2A crew to hold over the water, while they tried to pinpoint the downed pilot's position. Enemy MiG fighters, SAMs and AAA (anti-aircraft artillery) constantly harassed F-105s flying rescue combat air patrol (RESCAP) over Barnett. Thud pilots reported trucks headed for the area where Barnett had landed, adding yet another threat a SAR helicopter crew would encounter.

Then a Navy A-4B attacking another bridge north of Haiphong was hit by AAA, forcing Lieutenant Junior Grade Allan Perkins to eject over the harbor. He landed in shallow water less than a football field away from a cargo ship. Brennan's helicopter—call sign "Clementine"—was immediately dispatched to snag the downed Navy pilot. Threading ships anchored in the Haiphong harbor, the SAR crew eventually spotted a flare Perkins had fired. They pulled to a hover over the pilot and dropped a rescue swimmer, who had no idea Perkins was squatting or on his knees. Instead of splashing into deep water, the swimmer drove both finned feet into soft mud. Perkins helped free the SAR airman from harbor muck, so the two could be hoisted aboard. Clementine then managed to escape the harbor without incident.

By the time Perkins was delivered to his ship, daylight was fading fast and the UH-2A needed fuel. Steel Hawser "wouldn't let us go in at night to get Bob [Barnett]. He was told to hide and wait for rescue the next day," Jim recalls.

The same Clementine crew and two A-1 "Spads" found Barnett shortly after noon the following day—but North Vietnamese troops were waiting in ambush. By radio, Barnett guided the UH-2A to a hover directly above the fighter pilot. A forest penetrator was lowered, "But we couldn't get it down to him," Jim said. Despite the Spads doing their best to suppress bad-guy gunfire, the helicopter was subjected to a hailstorm of small arms rounds.

"I saw the fuel gauge go to zero and the annunciator panel light up," Jim said. One of the pilots called "Mayday! Mayday!" and turned toward the coast. They made it to the Gulf of Tonkin, before running out of fuel and ditching their bird 10 miles offshore.

Thanks to that weight-saving removal of flotation gear back in the Philippines, the UH-2A promptly sank—and rolled inverted. Jim unsnapped his shoulder harness and seat belt, kicked away from the armored seat and swam through the door to his left. As he paddled to the surface, Jim was struck by the profusion of holes he saw in the helicopter's underside.

THAT's why our fuel disappeared so fast!

A Navy SH-3 helicopter from a nearby aircraft carrier was soon overhead, plucking their SAR brethren from Haiphong harbor. By early afternoon, the Navy recalled its search and rescue forces and told the downed pilot he was looking at a second night in the bush, evading North Vietnamese hunting parties. Unfortunately, Barnett was captured the next day. When his captors ordered him to lure SAR aircraft into a flak trap, Barnett repeatedly called on the rescue channel, "This is Zark! I'm alive! Come get me!" That and other nonstandard radio ruses warned rescuers away from his position and enemy gunners. But Barnett was doomed to endure five and a half years of brutal treatment in North Vietnamese prisons.

For their Bob Barnett rescue attempts, Jim was awarded a Distinguished Flying Cross and his fellow pilot, Tim Mclecosky, received the Silver Star.

Jim logged six combat rescues, most under enemy fire, during his Southeast Asia tour of duty. While retrieving one pilot who had punched out, after his F-4 Phantom's flight controls failed, Jim's helicopter was subjected to a barrage of mortar fire. The HU-2A obviously was taking hits, but not until a postflight inspection did Jim realize shrapnel had blown a hole in the fuselage about one foot behind his head.

Luck and mere inches often determined who lived among the SAR community.

Like most SAR pilots of the era, Jim Brennan tends to downplay the fact that he and his fellow HC-7 Sea Devils routinely flew directly into deadly gunfire to rescue American warriors. They risked their lives so others might live. Some of those the Sea Devils rescued went on to serve America in other ways. One of many the squadron saved from captivity or death was fighter ace Randy "Duke" Cunningham, who later became a California congressman.

U.S. Navy UH-2A "Clementine" pilots Jim Brennan (back row, left end) and Tim Mclecosky (back row, right end) with their flight and ground crews, circa 1967.

Jim Brennan later flew training and other missions in Japan, before returning to Penascola Naval Air Station. He completed active duty as a North American T-28 "Trojan" flight instructor, but stayed in the Reserves and flew the Douglas C-118 transport. He joined a small commuter airline, before signing on as a pilot for American Airlines in 1973. The national economic downturn prompted a furlough from 1974 to November 1975, when he was recalled. Retiring from American in 2000, Jim switched to corporate aviation and flew the Gulfstream GIV and Cessna Citation X for Northrop Grumman until retiring again in 2009.

* "Ozark Lead is out of the aircraft"; W. Howard Plunkett, *Air Power History*, Spring 2005, p. 5.

PLAIN-DE-JARS BLOWOUT

Joseph A. Guthrie, Jr.

Early in 1968, after a bombing halt in the Plain-de-Jars had been lifted, Lieutenant Colonel Ralph Hoggatt and I were scheduled to fly our first mission into the area. Ralph had led an incredible rescue near the Mu Gia Pass on 11 November 1967, and ultimately was awarded the "Air Force Cross for extraordinary heroism that day when, for nearly an hour, he almost single-handedly faced overwhelming odds in one of the hottest areas of Southeast Asia."* A great pilot to have on my wing.

602nd Fighter Squadron (Commando) A-1E Skyraider
U.S. Air Force

Flying the single-engine, World War II-vintage Douglas A-1 *Skyraider*, Ralph and I were a little apprehensive about returning to yet another known hot spot. We had been warned that the area would be heavily re-fortified, because it had seen no hostile action for some time. This would be our unit's first incursion back there...and I was the designated flight lead. Consequently, I paid close attention to the briefing, taking particular note of where anti-aircraft gun emplacements might be located.

Designated *Firefly* flight, we took off and flew to the target without incident, looked it over carefully, and decided on the best run-in heading and escape route. I rolled in first, dropped a Mk. 82 500-pound bomb and reported minimal ground fire. So far, so good!

But as I pulled out from that first pass, I heard a loud explosion and felt a blast right under my posterior. I'd been hit! Hit in my most vital region! Every male aviator's nightmare! In a cold sweat, I unloaded to reduce g-loads and proceeded to investigate the damage. My *Spad* (the A-1's nickname) was now on an erratic flight path, prompting Ralph to ask whether I was in trouble. I was too involved with self-examination to respond.

No blood, no pain. I was not soprano. Good! *Very, very good!* I climbed to a safe altitude, then tried to figure out what the hell had happened.

The old prop-driven *Skyraider* was equipped with a Stanley Aviation Corporation-developed *Yankee* extraction system instead of an ejection seat. To escape, a pilot activated the system by pulling a handle to blow the canopy off and fire a rocket. Hooked to a series of straps and harness, the rocket system literally yanked you up and out of the aircraft, and deployed a parachute. But you had to sit on a hard seat pan all the time. After three or four hours, the old butt would really talk to you.

For relief, most pilots sat on an inner tube-like inflatable ring that had been liberated from hemorrhoid patients in the local hospital. These tail-relieving treasures were passed from pilot to pilot. We considered them of incalculable value and guarded each tube accordingly. However, constant usage in an environment for which they were clearly not designed tended to shorten the precious rings' life span.

Sure enough, just as I'd pulled off-target, the combination of age and repeated g-forces resulted in massive failure, blowing a fist-size hole in my hemorrhoid-protector inner-tube.

Flying back to Udorn, still worried that I had been hit, Ralph repeatedly asked about my condition. I replied—in my most resolute tenor voice—that I'd explain when we were on the ground. No way was I going to broadcast details over the air.

After landing, we shared a good laugh about at least one hilarious moment of our combat tour. And during the mission debriefing, I never mentioned being "hit".

* *Valor: Veterans Day, 1967; Air Force Magazine*, Dec. 1, 1991 (https://www.airforcemag.com/article/valor-veterans-day-1967/)

After graduating from the U.S. Military Academy at West Point in 1949, the late-Joe Guthrie was commissioned into the Army infantry. But he'd much rather be in the newly formed U.S. Air Force. A week following graduation, Joe wrote a request for transfer and walked it through the Pentagon. The request was turned down. Joe's classmate, Doug Bush, suffered the same fate, but as a veteran of World War II, he knew how to get things done. Doug talked his way into General Omar Bradley's living quarters and convinced Bradley to transfer him, Joe and four others to the Air Force. Thus began Joe's 28-year USAF career. He flew forward air controller missions during the Korean War and classified reconnaissance missions in early Cold War years. In the Vietnam War, Joe commanded the 602nd Fighter Squadron (Commando) at Udorn Air Base, Thailand, flying the A-1E on close air support, forward air control and Jolly Green rescue-helicopter escort missions. He later served as chief of test for the C-5A transport aircraft. From 1972 to 1975, Joe was commandant of the Air Force Test Pilot School at Edwards Air Force Base. His final active-duty assignment was as the U.S. Air Force Flight Test Center's deputy commander for operations (test wing commander) until he retired in 1977. He continued to fly as a test pilot and director of flight operations for the next 14 years, initially for American Jet Industries (now Gulfstream Aerospace Corporation), then Tracor Flight Systems. Joe was a fellow and past president of the Society of Experimental Test Pilots, and a member of the Montana Pilots Association, the Helena Hangar of Quiet Birdmen and myriad other military and aviation organizations.

COMBAT MISSION WITH DAD
Francis "Rusty"Gideon

My combat tour began with a C-130 crew dumping me on the sweltering taxiway at Phan Rang, Republic of Vietnam, home of the 35th Tactical Fighter Wing. A freshly minted 1st Lieutenant fighter pilot, I'd graduated from F-100 Super Sabre training in May 1968, then three successive survival schools, before being shipped overseas.

A jeep carrying two lieutenants wheeled up and stopped. "Hey, what unit are you assigned to?"

"Six-fifteenth Bobcats," I replied.

"Too bad. We saw you first. You're in the three-fifty-second Yellow Jackets now." Nice try, but I was checking in at the 615th by the next afternoon.

35th Tactical Fighter Wing F-100 flight
F-100.org

About the same time, my father, Lieutenant General Francis Gideon, was taking command of 13th Air Force, headquartered at Clark Air Force Base in The Philippines. Although he had no units in South Vietnam, a screwy command structure gave him administrative responsibility—but not operational control—of Air Force units in Thailand. A hands-on leader, who always wanted to see the war for himself, he grabbed every opportunity to visit his command's units in Thailand and Vietnam.

In February 1969, my father flew into Cam Rahn Bay (32 miles north of Phan Rang), and hitched a ride to Phan Rang with USAF security cops. A three-star general traveling through a war zone in a jeep seemed foolhardy to me, but he wanted to know what was going on in our area. He also wanted to fly a combat mission with me. Obviously, few pilots have an opportunity to fly in combat with family members, much less in the same airplane. This was the chance of a lifetime—but making it happen would require serious political wrangling.

In early 1968, Major General Bob Worley, Vice Commander of 7th Air Force, had been killed, while flying an RF-4C in Vietnam. Following that tragedy, 7th Air Force dictated that general officers (G.O.) would not fly in combat. That G.O.-no-fly policy was still in effect.

It turned out that General George Brown, 7th Air Force Commander, and my dad were good friends. And General Brown owned the 35th Wing, to which I was assigned. After pitching a few good reasons—needing to take a first-hand look at F-100's in action; understanding how the close air support (CAS) mission was being executed in South Vietnam, etc.—my father was cleared to fly a combat sortie with me. General Brown had one caveat: the flight was not to be publicized in any way, shape or form. In addition, my boss, Colonel Frank Gailer, 35th Tactical Fighter Wing commander, made it very clear that I'd "better not put any scratches on the general!"

Lt. Gen. Francis Gideon and his son, Capt. "Rusty" Gideon, ready to fly.
U.S. Air Force

Our father-son mission launched as a two-ship, with Captain Al Walker as flight lead. Dad and I were on Al's wing, flying a two-seat "F"-model F-100. Planned as a tree-buster in northern III Corps, not far from Phan Rang, the mission was not publicized, but everyone who came up on the radio that day knew who was in "Bobcat 12". Maybe "leaking" that info ensured General Brown had the last laugh, or he was making sure we didn't sneak off and partake of real combat.

Once in the mission area, a Forward Air Controller (FAC) identified a lucrative target, but restricted us to only dropping our slick M-117 bombs from above 3,000 feet. And no strafing allowed! We made our bomb run and the FAC reported a nice bomb damage assessment (BDA)—100 meters of trench destroyed, 50 meters of trench damaged, three fighting positions destroyed, six bunkers destroyed, and four bunkers damaged. He also threw in a profusion of attaboys for our stellar accuracy.

Truth be told, there wasn't a Viet Cong troop or anything more threatening than big trees within 50 miles of that place. Still, I'd logged a personally satisfying combat mission with my father, an honor rarely matched in the fighter community.

Lt. Gen. Francis Gideon and his son, "Rusty" Gideon
Rusty Gideon

In October 1996, long after my dad and General Brown had passed away, Air Force Magazine featured a "photo scrapbook" about the Vietnam War. One photo was of dad and me conducting the preflight, prior to our F-100 mission. It brought back good memories of that flight, a special, benchmark event for both of us. I only wish all my "Hun"-flying buddies could have had the same experience.

During a one-year combat tour in Vietnam, Major General "Rusty" Gideon (USAF, Ret.) flew 241 Close Air Support missions in the F-100 Super Sabre. He also flew the "Hun" and F-4 Phantom at RAF Lakenheath, United Kingdom, before returning to Vietnam. Flying the F-4E Phantom II, he escorted raids against North Vietnam, during a two-month tour in 1972. He then secured a Masters Degree in Systems Management from the Air Force Institute of Technology, followed by another year of graduate-level education at the USAF Test Pilot School. As a test pilot developing the A-10 "Warthog", he had the distinction of ejecting at low altitude, after both engines compressor stalled, during an A-10 gun-gas test. Subsequent assignments included System Command headquarters staff; various System Program Offices; commanding the Wright Patterson Air Force Base test wing; commander of Foreign Technology Division, the U.S. Air Force's Technical Intelligence Center; Vice Commander, Sacramento Air Logistics Center, and Director of Operations and Test for USAF Materiel Command. As the USAF Chief of Safety, he later commanded the Air Force Safety Center. He retired in 2000, having logged pilot time in more than 30 types of aircraft. As a safety consultant, he devoted two years to NASA's Return to Flight Program, following the space shuttle Challenger accident.

FREEDOM LAND

Randy DeAngelis

Lockheed Martin

As our Lockheed C-141 StarLifter left the Hickam Air Force Base (AFB), Hawaii, runway, the blue Pacific contrasted sharply with the islands' lush green vegetation, colors accentuated even more by a sun-drenched spring day. We were heavy. Our fuel tanks were full, and we had a cabin loaded with people prepared for a long, but very special flight.

Switching to departure frequency, I notified the controller we were climbing through 1,000 feet.

"MAC 60638, radar contact. Cleared direct Fort Smith," he answered crisply. That was a pleasant surprise for the entire crew. After flying around the Pacific region for 22 days, we now were cleared for a direct flight to Fort Smith, Arkansas. Maybe we'd even make it on home to Charleston this time.

The unusual clearance also surprised airliner crews in the area. They immediately started requesting similar direct-to-destination clearances. Everybody headed for the mainland hoped to save fuel and time, and a direct route was the most efficient. But their requests were rejected. The commercial flights were told to stay on their standard Hawaiian tracks. One airline pilot complained miserably, prompting the controller to finally explain the significance of our night mission. The grumbling pilot had no further comments.

We climbed quickly to our initial eastbound cruising altitude of 33,000 feet. Behind us, the Sun slipped below an orange-and-blue Hawaiian horizon, while the edge of night—sometimes called "The Terminator"—crept toward our StarLifter's nose. Cleared direct, the airspace ahead of us unobstructed—except for a few Midwestern thunderstorms down the road—our two navigators set us on-course. The cockpit was quiet, as each crewmember went about settling in for an eight-hour flight. A loadmaster checked in via interphone to report that all 154 of our passengers were quiet...and happy. He wondered whether we'd be going on home, or be turned back to Hickam for yet another airlift of Vietnamese refugees. And he wondered for good reason. This crew had crossed the dateline six times in the last seven days.

During the previous three weeks, we'd been an integral part of the inglorious U.S. departure and evacuation of Vietnam. Almost every one of our 22 days in April and May of 1975 had been devoted to ferrying people fleeing their homeland. We'd flown them from Saigon to Andersen Air Force Base, Guam, and Clark AFB in the Philippines; to Hickam AFB, Hawaii, then on to Ft. Smith, Arkansas, and camps in Pennsylvania. Many fled their homes with only the shirts on their backs. Others carried gold bars under their coats. All left family, homes, jobs and farms, fearing for their lives or just wanting to be free.

We'd shuttled from Vietnam in daylight and darkness, mission after mission. At times, we had departed Vietnam with countless numbers of refugees strapped to the aircraft's floor, racing to get airborne, before taking enemy fire. The notion of departing under an honorable peace had been reduced to simply rescuing a lucky few, bringing them to freedom. Some of those we carried may have appeared in that graphic photo of a rescue helicopter struggling to liftoff from atop the U.S. embassy.

Today, 46 years later, my neighbor is one of those who left Vietnam as a teenager. Perhaps we carried him to Ft. Smith that night. Perhaps we carried a lot of people who are now neighbors to hundreds of Americans.

In April 1975, though, the nation's mood was not so neighborly. The shock of seeing a president resign under a cloud, a years-long conflict in Southeast Asia, and a slumping economy were not conducive to American tolerance or open-armed acceptance of a large influx of yet another ethnic community. Even Congress, acting just six days prior to our night-flight, had rejected President Ford's request for resettlement funds. Those monies would have supported the very people we were carrying to America.

The administration had initially estimated the number of refugees at only 40,000, and had considered settling displaced Vietnamese in the Pacific Territories, where "their skills could be utilized," according to a spokesman. But within the first few days of evacuation, at least that number appeared to be living in tents on Andersen AFB. Thousands more were housed at Clark in the Philippines. Eventually, more than 120,000 fled the looming overcast of communism.

Even as the debate about what to do with them intensified at home, refugees flowed through Hickam AFB, buying new clothes in preparation for the next leg of their flight to freedom. Tonight, another group crossed the Pacific on smooth air, as a blanket of darkness crept over us.

Soon, from our stepped-up altitude of 37,000 feet, the glow of Los Angeles appeared. It was a clear night in Southern California, and the amber lights of that busy city and its surrounding suburbs pulsed with life—the throb of a huge, glowing organism. Crowded freeways were capillaries of red and white lights carrying the City of Angels' lifeblood. Those citizens, unaware of our presence above, went about life as free people do on any spring evening. It felt good to be over our home continent again.

Passing Los Angeles, we looked beyond its mountainous boundary into the dark deserts of eastern California and Arizona. The lights of Phoenix glowed on the horizon to our right. Another Military Airlift Command flight checked in with Albuquerque Center. Asking its crew to come up on an air-to-air frequency, we learned that the flight had just left Fort Smith and was headed back to Hickam for another load. They were from McGuire AFB, New Jersey, and had been flying Hickam-to-mainland shuttles for about a week.

"Yeah, we were hoping to go home, but at least ATC has given us direct-Hickam," the pilot radioed.

We had a visual on him now, off to our left about two miles and 2,000 ft.

below us. "In that case, you're right of course!" I chided, a weak attempt at pilot-humor.

"How long have you guys been out? You going home after this one?" the other MAC pilot queried.

"Twenty-two days," I replied. "Don't know. I guess we'll find out when we get there."

"Well, good luck," he said, preparing to sign off. "By the way, pull up the ADF (Automatic Direction Finder) in about twenty minutes. Ford has a news conference coming up. There's been a lot of backlash about us bringing all these people in."

We concluded by taking note of his pirep [pilot report] about thunderstorms in Oklahoma, Texas and Arkansas.

His comment concerning the growing backlash against Vietnamese refugees bothered me. I thought about my own grandparents—Italian immigrants—coming to America through Ellis Island at the turn of the century, seeking a better life and opportunities in America. My then-17-year-old grandfather, unable to speak English, had left 11 brothers and sisters behind. Within two years, he'd been drafted and sent back to Europe during World War I, wearing an American uniform and charged with defending the opportunity he had yet to realize. I was only one generation removed from his experience. Like many immigrant families, four generations of mine would ultimately serve during wartime—my grandfather in World War I, my father in World War II, me during Vietnam, and, three decades after that night C-141 mission, my son in the war against terror, serving in both Iraq and Afghanistan.

I cranked up the ADF, searching the frequency-bands for a strong-signal commercial radio broadcast by lightly turning the system's tuning crank. Thunderstorms were beginning to explode on the horizon, their cloud-to-cloud lightning silhouetting white popcorn-shaped clouds against a black sky. Weather-induced interference across the radio-frequency spectrum had almost convinced me to give up, when suddenly, a clear signal appeared. Where the station was located, I still don't know. President Ford's press conference had already begun, and ironically, the topic of Vietnamese refugees was now in our headsets.

Ford answered a number of questions about the Vietnam war. Then a reporter from the Chicago Daily News asked, "Mr. President, you have been reported as being 'damn mad' about the adverse reaction of the American people to Vietnam's refugees. How do you explain that?"

The president responded that yes, he was upset. America is a country built by immigrants from all over the world, he noted, and this has always been a humanitarian nation.

For a moment, my mind strayed from the broadcast. I felt deep concern for the people we were bringing to America. Their spirits had been so high when they boarded in Hawaii. Their dreams of freedom were about to be realized, and their hopes of a new life about to be fulfilled. And yet, they might walk off this airplane into the arms of bigotry, bias and discrimination.

The president continued his response, naming mayors and governors who supported giving these refugees a new opportunity. Since 60 percent were children, he believed the vast majority of Americans also wanted to give these people another chance. I felt better, knowing I served a President who could get "damn mad" about this issue, and who had not forgotten about my nation's roots.

The radio station's signal faded out. It had lasted just long enough to soothe the souls of our crew, airmen trying to find some kind of redeeming value in the unsettled conclusion of that long Vietnam conflict. Then the Arkansas skies parted, shown on our weather radar as clear passageways among the storms. We landed uneventfully in Fort Smith and taxied to the ramp.

Our passengers deplaned quickly via the rear cargo doors. But as I made a slow, tired descent from the flight deck into the cabin, I noticed a few refugees near the front were still gathering their meager belongings. A young Vietnamese father saw me, turned and said something to his wife and their four stair-step children. All six lined-up, turned toward me and, in unison, bowed a "thank you."

To my right, all the way forward, a young man—a teenager, perhaps—was still seated, looking up at me with a huge smile. Colorful in his new blue-jeans and Hawaiian shirt, he patted the aircraft floor with the palm of his right hand, proclaiming, "Freedom Land! Freedom Land!"

The author, Randy DeAngelis, retired after 23 years of active and reserve service with the U.S. Navy and U.S. Air Force, and following 31 years of service with United Airlines as Chief Pilot, Check Airman and Boeing 777 International Captain. He is now an Aviation Consultant on Unmanned Aircraft and Advanced Air Mobility.

COMBAT CONTRAILS: VIETNAM is the first book in a series of true stories ranging from the Cold War and reconnaissance to flight testing, combat in Iraq and Afghanistan, and special operations around the world. Readers interested in having their stories included in subsequent books should submit them or queries via the Contact sections of

www.williambscott.com or northslopepublications.com

Also from North Slope Publications:

**Rogue Cops:
You Kill. You Lie. You Die.**

"A thriller, chock full of high tech weapons and flying that only someone who has lived it...could write." 5 stars — Stephen Coonts

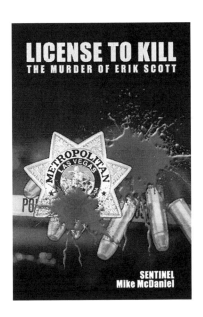

ACKNOWLEDGMENTS

A heartfelt thanks to the veterans who graciously shared their stories, some of which only survive in warriors' memories. Breaking decades of silence to recall sometimes-painful experiences of ground and aerial combat took courage and a commitment to ensuring their truths are not lost. To a man, all chose to tell their stories so families, friends, fellow warriors and every American citizen will know how their tours "in country" transpired.

Maybe current and future generations will read their accounts and appreciate the sacrifices made by these 18 men and thousands of their compatriots, young Americans who fought in Southeast Asia for a simple reason: Their nation called.

Once again, a world of gratitude and deep appreciation go to Tony and Shari Kern and their North Slope Publications team of pros for sharing a belief that American warriors' stories must be told. Aided by Lisa Caputo's amazing artistic talents and years of designing layouts for the world's premier aerospace magazine, North Slope Publications has transformed a collection of tales into a book that will be treasured by millions of veterans.

My profound, sincere THANK YOUs to Tony, Shari, Lisa and every veteran whose story appears herein.

—*William B. Scott*
June 2021